ALSO BY FRANK O'DEA

*When All You Have Is Hope*

D
Nex
Th

# Do the Next Right Thing

## Surviving Life's Crises

## FRANK O'DEA

With John Lawrence Reynolds

VIKING

VIKING
an imprint of Penguin Canada

Published by the Penguin Group
Penguin Group (Canada), 90 Eglinton Avenue East, Suite 700, Toronto, Ontario, Canada M4P 2Y3

Penguin Group (USA) Inc., 375 Hudson Street, New York, New York 10014, U.S.A.
Penguin Books Ltd, 80 Strand, London WC2R 0RL, England
Penguin Ireland, 25 St Stephen's Green, Dublin 2, Ireland (a division of Penguin Books Ltd)
Penguin Group (Australia), 707 Collins Street, Melbourne, Victoria 3008, Australia
(a division of Pearson Australia Group Pty Ltd)
Penguin Books India Pvt Ltd, 11 Community Centre, Panchsheel Park, New Delhi—110 017, India
Penguin Group (NZ), 67 Apollo Drive, Rosedale, Auckland 0632, New Zealand
(a division of Pearson New Zealand Ltd)
Penguin Books (South Africa) (Pty) Ltd, 24 Sturdee Avenue, Rosebank,
Johannesburg 2196, South Africa

Penguin Books Ltd, Registered Offices: 80 Strand, London WC2R 0RL, England

First published 2013

1 2 3 4 5 6 7 8 9 10 (RRD)

Author representation: Westwood Creative Artists
94 Harbord Street, Toronto, Ontario M5S 1G6

Excerpts from *The Third Man Factor* by John Geiger used with permission.

Manufactured in the U.S.A.

LIBRARY AND ARCHIVES CANADA CATALOGUING IN PUBLICATION

O'Dea, Frank, author
Do the next right thing : surviving life's crises /
Frank O'Dea with John Lawrence Reynolds.

ISBN 978-0-670-06587-5

1. Self-actualization (Psychology). 2. Change (Psychology).
I. Reynolds, John Lawrence, author II. Title.

BF637.S4O34 2013      158.1      C2013-903761-6

Visit the Penguin Canada website at **www.penguin.ca**

Special and corporate bulk purchase rates available; please see
**www.penguin.ca/corporatesales** or call 1-800-810-3104, ext. 2477.

**ALWAYS LEARNING**                                                **PEARSON**

# Contents

# Introduction

I have learned many secrets in life, but perhaps the most valuable is one that often appears difficult to understand and apply.

The secret is this: *The whole of your life's experience is but an outer expression of your inner thoughts.* Your life at the moment, whether fruitful and fulfilling or empty and tragic, reflects the choices you have made in the past. We choose how we think, and in turn, the way we think influences the choices we make that shape our lives. We have free will, but the way we use our free will is a direct result of the thoughts we choose to have.

Neither my life nor yours has been an accident. They have been the result of choices you and I have made.

This book is about making choices to enhance the experience of life. The choices are not mine to suggest, to own, or to make on your behalf. They are yours to select, to acquire, and to use. They are simple to understand and easy to apply, and they have been used by many people with great success. Yet the core of my idea will appear revolutionary to some people. Which, I suppose, could lead to me being labeled a rebel.

I have been labeled a number of things in my life, especially during that part of my life before I overcame my addiction to alcohol. None of the labels was flattering, and I have no doubt that the people who applied them to me believed they were permanent, or at least suitable for the long run. They included *drunk*, *loser*, *bum*, and the usual epithets handed out to people who appear to have a disastrous past, an appalling present, and a bleak future.

If it need be said, I am none of those today. I am a successful businessman, an attentive husband, the proud father of two active and often challenging daughters, and a guy dedicated to offering assistance to those in need of mentors and cheerleaders. Writing about my journey from homeless alcoholic to my current status added another identity: bestselling author. My book *When All You Have Is Hope* changed the lives of hundreds, perhaps thousands of people. Many of them wrote to tell me of their hardships, and of how my book assisted them in overcoming their problems. Of all the things I may achieve in my life, none will give me more pride and satisfaction than knowing I improved the lives of strangers through my book and my public speaking.

Some of the stories in this book have been derived from those letters. I have changed the names and a few of the circumstances to respect the privacy of those who wrote to me, but the essence remains. Their stories, and their difficulties in dealing with some of the challenges facing them, inspired this book.

So what's all this talk about being a revolutionary? Simply this: Much of the success of Western society is based on the idea of taking immediate action, as in, "Don't just stand there—do something!" *And that is often precisely the wrong thing to do.*

Leaping into action makes obvious sense when your house is engulfed in flames, or when a mad bull comes charging at you across an open meadow. But let's face it: Almost none of the personal crises you and I will encounter in our lives has any relation to these kinds of events. The truth is that it is best not to act immediately in the midst of a crisis situation that does not involve three-alarm fires or angry bulls. Do we need to take action? Of course we do. *But only if we do the next right thing*.

The idea of not acting in the face of a crisis is the revolutionary concept I'm proposing in this book. At first glance it appears to fly in the face of much we have been taught. Upon hearing my idea, some people assume that I am suggesting they abdicate their responsibilities when dealing with a personal crisis. Well, I'm not. I am not suggesting that you do nothing, nor am I suggesting that you do something. The title of the book, after all, suggests neither of these things. It is *Do the Next Right Thing*. The core problem many of us fail to overcome is that we cannot identify the next right thing to do. Why? *Because in the midst of a crisis situation, we are the least qualified person to recognize just what it is we should do*.

Let me explain, with an actual incident that occurred shortly before I sat down to write this book.

Among the most satisfying volunteer work I do is sponsoring recovering alcoholics and those facing various other challenges, such as trying to integrate themselves into society under difficult circumstances. Like Darren.*

Darren had suffered an appalling childhood, one that he will likely spend his life overcoming. Filled with anger at memories of abuse, he fell into alcoholism and petty crime while still in his teens. By his twenties, he had acquired a family that represented the best part of his life: a wife who clearly cared for him, and two children to whom he wanted to give a better life than the one he had experienced.

Good intentions, as we all know, are never enough on their own. Darren served a prison sentence as a result of his criminal actions and I agreed to sponsor him in a counseling group when he was released from jail. My assistance would be limited to providing guidance on how to stay off alcohol and generally being a source of support when he felt he needed it. His biggest challenges, along with staying off alcohol, were controlling his anger and finding a job.

One day, after a session with the counseling group, I offered Darren a ride home. We chatted about nothing in particular until, not far from his home, he asked me to stop at a convenience store for a moment. He had deposited a welfare check for $1000 in his account that day, and the convenience store had an ATM where Darren planned to withdraw enough cash to purchase groceries for his family.

While Darren entered the store I waited in the car, listening to the radio and relaxing. No more than a few minutes had passed

---

* As I mentioned, I have changed people's names, so this is not his real name. The incident, however, is very real, as are the other examples in this book.

when I was startled to see the door to the convenience store swing open with enough force to almost tear it off its hinges and Darren emerge, striding toward my car. It wasn't the violently opening door that disturbed me. It was the angry expression on Darren's face.

"It took my bank card!" Darren almost shouted at me. "The damn machine ate my card and won't give it back! How am I gonna get cash and buy groceries for my wife and kids? How're we gonna pay the rent and the hydro bill and everything else if I don't get the card back? *We'll be out on the damn street!*"

After persuading him to calm down, I listened as Darren described what had occurred inside the convenience store. While it might have qualified as a silly nuisance to some—the refusal of the ATM to return a card it may have suspected was stolen or being used in a fraudulent transaction or just due to a mechanical glitch—it was a serious crisis to Darren. In his mind all the abuses he had suffered as a child were being directed at him again, this time by a damn machine.

Darren had reacted in the only way he knew how. He had shouted, he had raged, he had applied physical force to the machine with a couple of kicks. The only response was from the store manager, who, alarmed by Darren's actions, warned that he was prepared to call 911 and ask for the police, an action that would have sent Darren back to jail.

Fortunately, Darren didn't act entirely in his usual fashion. Recalling advice I had given him about dealing with difficult situations, he left the store and came out to my car, an action that I am convinced he would not have taken a few weeks earlier. Instead of resorting to the only response that Darren's experience had taught him, which was to lash out at anyone or anything that stood in his way, Darren came to speak with me and, at my suggestion, agreed to follow me back into the store.

At the sight of Darren, the store manager's eyes widened and he took a step closer to his telephone.

"We seem to have a problem with your machine," I said to the manager with a smile. Then, noting a sticker on the ATM listing a telephone number to call in case of difficulties, I entered the number on my cell phone, contacted a pleasant individual at the bank, and explained the situation.

It was all, of course, a misunderstanding. The wrong PIN or a computer fault at the bank had triggered a programmed response leading to Darren's near meltdown. Within minutes we had Darren's card back, some cash dispensed, and food for his family's dinner in the backseat of my car. It had all been a mere nuisance. Except for Darren. To him, it had been a crisis.

Faced with a similar situation, you may have known instinctively the next right thing to do: Call the number on the machine, explain things to a representative, and wait for the matter to clear up.

But you're not Darren. You likely don't have a background that includes twenty years of ill-treatment, a prison record, a reservoir of anger lurking beneath the surface, and a sense that the world will never give you a fair shake because ... well, just because it's you. That's what Darren had to deal with. When the ATM pulled the kind of mechanical glitch that many of us can shrug off, Darren was not equipped to do the next right thing *because he didn't know what he needed to do.* He knew only what his emotions told him, which was to fight back against an unjust world. Darren is not a stupid man, but for a minute or two, when he felt the ATM was defying him for reasons of its own, he became intellectually incapable of dealing with the situation.

He needed to step away from the situation.

He needed to find someone or something to trust.

He needed to find the peace that would enable him to recognize the next right thing to do.

*Then* he needed to do the next right thing. Immediate action was the last thing he needed to take.

The lesson, as simple as it sounds, is one we need to learn and heed when faced with any of the unknown and unexpected personal crises we will face in our lives. We need to:

- place our trust in a safe place
- find peace
- do the next right thing.

ONE

# Lessons from Life:
# Mine and Others'

*To live your life is not as simple as to cross a field.*
—BORIS PASTERNAK, *DOCTOR ZHIVAGO*

I have told this tale so often that I almost feel it is someone else's story. But it is all mine, and only the passage of time and frequent retelling give me the sense that I am distanced from it. In fact, I am not. It is a part of me and always will be.

Briefly, here is my story:

*I am twenty-four years old. I am a homeless alcoholic and the victim of sexual abuse as a teenager. Three days before Christmas, I stand shivering on a midtown street corner, hoping to beg enough money to purchase a bottle of wine. This represents the limit of my ambition: I will be successful enough to persuade strangers to part with a few coins they won't miss, enabling me to buy something that*

*I believe will help me survive the day. I will worry about tomorrow some other time.*

I did not know it then, but on that day just before Christmas I had reached a crisis point. The point arrived when I realized I could not continue living the same way I had been living for the past few years. If I did, I would die on the streets. It could happen the next day, the next week, or the next month, but it would surely happen soon, and nobody would care.

I had known this for several months. Now I was acknowledging it as the truth. But acknowledgment isn't enough, because acknowledgment isn't action. I needed to take action. I just didn't know what to do. Or how to do it.

Most people believe that crises descend upon them suddenly and unexpected, like lightning. One moment you are strolling down the sidewalk on a bright, sunny day, and the next moment a piano falls ten floors down onto your head. But crises rarely happen in such an unexpected manner. They tend to build right in front of your eyes although you may be unable to recognize their presence until you're forced to deal with them.

The major challenge you'll face in dealing with personal crises is not an inability to take action. In fact, it is almost always exactly the opposite: People take action at a time when they should not be doing anything at all, because whatever they choose on the spur of the moment will almost certainly be the wrong thing to do. Doing the wrong thing will never resolve whatever crisis you have encountered. It is far more likely to extend the crisis situation and make it worse.

The biggest crisis I have faced in my life arrived on that frigid day in December. It did not come from the sky or from the actions of others. It originated inside my own head. As I stood hunched up against the cold, holding out one hand to receive whatever money people chose to put in it while keeping the other hand in my pocket to avoid frostbitten fingers, I heard a voice speak to me. It was my own voice, and it said: *If I don't change, I will die this way, and very soon.*

It had to be a total change, not just some small adjustment. The change would turn me into somebody I had never been before. If I wanted to pull it off (and while I was determined to try, I doubted whether I could), I would have to stop drinking. Not just today or tomorrow, but forever. I would set goals for myself, which I had done in the past, but this time I would have to achieve them and not make up excuses when I failed. I would have to find work and earn enough income to be self-sufficient. I would have to abandon my street buddies, the only friends I had. I would have to achieve more in the next few weeks than I had achieved in my entire life. And I would have to do all of this without relying on anyone else for support. My family had lost all hope that I would ever change, and I couldn't blame them. I had gone to them in the past, promising to change, and then breaking those promises to them and to myself. This time it would be just me.

During my years of alcohol addiction it had become clear to me that I would not be able to change things alone. That was a goal I knew would be impossible to achieve. On its own, the knowledge that you need to change your life is not enough to overcome the need to keep consuming whatever you are addicted to until you enter a crisis mode. When the need to change became overwhelming to me—when it essentially threatened my life—I entered a crisis stage.

If someone, knowing I had just experienced this epiphany, had seized me by the arm that day and said, "What you have to do is just stop drinking," this would have been the obvious action. But it would have been the *wrong* thing to do. My entire life revolved around alcohol. On that basis, giving up alcohol would have been equal to giving up on life. Trying to end my alcoholism in this manner would have produced a total failure on my part because I would have told myself, "Just one more drink," and fallen back into the same doomed cycle. Having tried and failed, I would have had even less self-respect and would have attempted to overcome it with more drinking. Later, the same realization that I would die drunk in the gutter would have overwhelmed me, and once again I would have sworn off alcohol only to desperately want a drink within a few days, a few hours—and then I'd have felt even worse when I did. This was a cycle with which I was too familiar.

I could not do it alone. I needed a Higher Power to assist me.

Many people assume "Higher Power" refers to God or whatever source of religious faith and spiritual strength they choose to follow. In my case, raised as a Roman Catholic, I might have sought strength there. But I couldn't. As a teenager, I had been abused by two priests on separate occasions. It may be possible for some people to ignore experiences like those and still retain their faith in the Church as a source of guidance and protection, but it was impossible for me at that time. I had to find my Higher Power elsewhere.

I found it among a group of people who understood my situation, and who were dedicated to providing the power I needed. In their hands I found something more than advice and support. I found peace. Having found peace, I knew what needed to be done, and what could be done without fear of failure.

The group invested time, energy, and even money in assisting me and others like me to escape alcohol addiction, because they knew how destructive it can be and how hard it is to abandon. They knew because the group members had gone through the same process themselves. They didn't respond to my situation with the usual condemnations like "Get a job!" or "Shape up!" or "Just stop drinking!" This kind of advice would have been the wrong thing to offer, and any attempt by me to obey them would have been doomed to fail.

They also knew the importance of using a proven method to deal with a major crisis by breaking it down to a series of small steps. Change my life overnight? Boy, that's a challenge. Take one small step today and another step tomorrow? I just might be able to do that. And I did.

This was one of the most important lessons I acquired. There is almost never a single perfect solution to the crises you encounter in life. There are always, however, smaller things—the next right thing—that can be done on your way to resolving the risk, the pain, and the fears you face.


That's how I overcame my addiction to alcohol, which was the root of my crisis. I had many reasons for explaining why I had chosen to deal with things by living in an alcoholic haze, but I couldn't lean on them as though they were crutches. I had been doing that for years. They had long ago ceased to be explanations and had become excuses for not changing. I had reasons to change now. I just wasn't sure how.

The series of steps I cover in this book worked for me as they have worked over many years for millions of people like me who were caught in an addiction to alcohol. Giving ourselves the same advice that others often shouted to us—"Sober up and stop drinking!"—sounded like a good idea. But it would have been the wrong thing to do. Give us a little step we can take today, a means of reassuring ourselves that we are making progress, and the promise of a bright new day ahead, and maybe we can make it. Having done it, we can recognize the next right thing to do and do it.

Those steps led to more than a way out of the trap of alcoholism that had ensnared me for much of my life. It led me to successfully launching and managing, and later selling my shares in, Second Cup—among the first of the gourmet coffee chains in North America—for a substantial amount of money. From there I moved to owning and operating a series of successful businesses, founding charitable organizations such as Street Kids International and Night of a Thousand Dinners, marrying a woman who believed in me and in all that I might accomplish, and experiencing fatherhood with two very bright and lively daughters. Along the way I earned various forms of recognition, including induction as an Officer of the Order of Canada.

The one-step-at-a-time process works for me, obviously. But would it work for others as well? After all, not everyone (thankfully) suffers from alcohol addiction. But everyone faces crises in their lives from time to time, and can use assistance to deal with them. Some challenges are minor irritations. Others may threaten your security, your happiness, and your well-being. Moving beyond your crises is necessary, but asking you simply to do this is like asking alcoholics simply to move beyond their addiction. They are *here* and they want to get over *there*. But *there* is on the other side of a deep, wide chasm, and the distance is too far to reach in a single leap.

Nearly forty years have passed since I stood at a crossroad in my life similar to the ones experienced by people in this book. Perhaps that crossroad is similar to the one you find yourself occupying today. I found help to deal with my crisis and lift me out of the gutter and into the life I enjoy now. It's only fair that I share with others the things I have learned from my experiences, then and over the years of building a life I could only have dreamed of in those days of shivering on street corners. I have done so in my community and charitable activities, and now I am sharing them in this book.

In the years since my book *When All You Have Is Hope* appeared, I have met with and spoken about my experience to thousands of people across North America. Many shared the personal crises they once faced, and how they managed to cope with them. I listened to their stories, many of them similar to my experiences before, during, and after my life on the street. That's when I began to see the solution that has always been there, yet has been out of sight to many of us because we were unable to view it correctly. The things that people told me about their lives, their fears, and their challenges were always touching, frequently inspiring, and sometimes dismaying.

The inspiring messages included this one from Catherine, a high school student:

> *I have troubles in my life at the moment regarding my family. Not as horrible as your life was, but I still found a connection to your story after reading it.... I am truly honoured for your willingness to share your life journey with the world around you, and I am very grateful that your pursuing of hope has inspired me to continue to believe that I will always have the power to change ...*

One of the stories I told in *When All You Have Is Hope* concerned the depression I suffered when I realized that I had been outmaneuvered in gaining control of Second Cup, and my reaction might have been construed as that of someone whose interest was rooted entirely in succeeding at a business venture. A woman named Linda disagreed. Hearing me discuss the situation and my reaction prompted her to write:

> *I realized [Frank] was talking about how I felt when I went through a divorce after thirty-two years of marriage. I never realized that a person leaving a company could experience the same hardships as someone going through a divorce. His words were very comforting.*

My story appears to have affected women more than men. Or perhaps women feel more comfortable expressing their deepest emotions than men do. In any case, a woman named Cheryl wrote to say she had been moved to tears by my story—the part in which I wrote about seeking the assistance I knew I needed from a Higher Power. I had approached the counseling group unsure of how I would be received and whether I indeed could be assisted; the first woman I encountered responded to my plea, "I need help," by saying, "You're home." A member of the group became my personal counselor, and at our first meeting he gave me a handful of dimes (this was long before cell phones, at a time when one thin dime worked in pay telephones), telling me to call him anytime I felt an overwhelming desire to have a drink. He promised to offer support and help me resist the urge. "You found hope in a handful of dimes," Cheryl commented, and I have never heard a better description of the assistance I needed to deal with my crisis.

I have a file drawer full of similar letters from people who took the time to locate my address and give me their response to my book. Their letters revealed that many people seek assistance in finding happiness in their lives, and much of this assistance comes from learning that others have faced similar circumstances, and overcome them.

Not all the letters I received brought happy endings with them. A man named Bill, who had worked in social services for more than twenty years, assisting others in their personal crises, found himself facing one of his own:

*I am in new territory for the first time. I have been*
*unemployed for over a year ... lost my relationship ...*
*lost my home and everything I felt was important to me.*

*I have moved to a different city to ground myself again and try to rebuild. It has been the hardest thing I have ever experienced. I understand now how all those people I worked with over the years ended up where they did ... it's only my life skills and some family support that have allowed me to exist and not fall in so many ways.*

*I am working to get my career going but I am stuck ... not sure where to go or what to do.... It's a strange feeling—one day you're onstage talking in front of hundreds of people, sitting at tables with CEOs, MPs, and mayors, and the next day you're a nobody.*

Stories such as Bill's convinced me to put all that I had learned about handling personal crises into another book. Instead of relating stories of the things I had endured, I would explain the hard lessons I acquired while dealing with and surviving those things. More important, I would provide the means for others to follow the proven path I have trod over many years.

One of the terms used to describe how people feel in the midst of a crisis is that they are in *free fall*. Dropping from one place to another, they are unsure how long they will fall, where they will land, and whether they will survive the landing. The only thing they believe for certain is that they have little or no control over this unwelcome journey.

Believing you lack control over your own life is a major cause of depression. That's not just my opinion, by the way. It is a fact confirmed by psychologists. Many people whose stories you will read about in this book are depressed for precisely that reason. After having lost a spouse, a relationship, a job, or some other part of their identity, they believe they have no control over the future they face. So it stands to reason that the most effective method of rising out of a depressed state caused by a personal crisis is to retrieve control of our lives.

That's a simple suggestion for a complex process. Among the symptoms of depression is having difficulty taking meaningful action to deal with the situation. Question: How can you take control of your life when your life is controlling you? Answer: By letting go. By finding the place where you are above and beyond the reaches of your crisis. By recognizing, from this new point of view, what must be done and having the confidence, the assurance, and the total certainty of doing it.

And sometimes by having the support of someone who knows what you are going through and, even more important, knows how to help you through it. Here are two more letters I received from people who learned of my story:

*Dear Frank:*

*The other day I walked into a bookstore intending to purchase a certain book I wanted to read. On the way I noticed the title of your book,* When All You Have Is Hope. *It caught me by surprise. I didn't plan to purchase and read it but now that I have, I need to write you.*

*You see, we both have a lot in common. The first thing we have in common is coffee. You established your business success and your identity through launching the Second Cup chain of coffee shops, and I have always enjoyed and relied on coffee to give me a "lift" to my day ...*

*The second point we have in common is that we were once homeless addicts, and that's where your book really touched me. I don't know about you but I'm a little ashamed that I fell into a certain lifestyle like I did. Even though everything since then has changed, I still think about my previous life every day. Unlike you, however, I remain in the closet with my past.*

*I am part of a highly successful group of entrepreneurs today. When I was in my early twenties I was lying semiconscious on a park bench at the same time that the other entrepreneurs were getting their feet wet for the first time as businesspeople.*

*That's why the part of your book describing how you overcame the challenges in your life resonated with me so strongly. I guess you could say that your book came at the perfect time.*

*GW*

*Dear Mr. O'Dea:*

*I am writing to let you know that I am here today because I heard you speak at a business conference some time ago.*

*At the time my wife had left me, I had lost the house, and my car was repossessed literally the day before I went to the conference. My children wouldn't speak to me and I was barely holding on to my job in the insurance business. All of my problems, I'm sure you have figured out, were*

*linked to my inability to deal with my drinking*
*problem.*

*When I heard you speak, and discovered that you not*
*only managed to overcome your alcoholism but also achieved*
*great success as a businessman, I realized that my problems*
*were not insurmountable. I continue to struggle every day*
*to keep my craving for alcohol under control, but I no longer*
*harbor suicidal thoughts and I have recovered my*
*self-esteem ...*

*A.H.K*

In thinking about crises and the people who shared their stories with me, I was reminded of the proverb that says: *He who takes a family gives hostages to fortune.* (It also works when you replace "he" with "she," by the way.) It's a reminder that we cannot escape actions that we cannot control. It also teaches us that the more we invest in life's happiness, the more we risk losing it whenever we encounter a crisis that we cannot handle.

As the file of letters built up, I realized that while my book addressed alcoholism specifically, each day millions of people were grappling with events in their lives that had nothing directly to do with drinking.

Many stories related to crises beyond addiction, and the need to deal with them was vital to the people who told me their tales. They were rooted in events that everyone faces at one point or another in their lives, sometimes simultaneously—the dissolution of a marriage, the loss of a job, the death of a spouse, and many more. Only a minority of people, thank God, find themselves deeply addicted to alcohol and drugs, but personal crises happen to everyone, and there are various means of dealing with them.

So it occurred to me one day: Is there a predictable means of dealing successfully with a personal crisis? Can a process be developed that gives everyone guidance on moving through a crisis as quickly and painlessly as possible?

I'm not speaking of the kind of event associated with serious mental disorders leading to suicidal tendencies; these disorders require treatment by qualified professionals. What I'm referring to is the kind of common but serious events you may bump up against in your life even when you're mentally healthy. These events are unexpected, and appear to defy your ability to deal with them. They can be merely irritating and temporary, or they can be painful, debilitating, and frightening.

Based on my experiences and on studies of various methods of dealing with crises, I became aware that I had been practicing my own means of tackling the problem for years. The method had grown naturally out of decisions I made many years ago, first when I chose to take charge of my life, and later when I consciously applied a step-by-step process to make it all happen.

In the midst of a severe crisis, you seek the same things you look for when suffering a severe headache—quick relief from the agony, and resumption of your peaceful and generally pain-free life. Few pain relievers work so quickly and thoroughly, and few solutions to our crises provide similar one-step effects. The process involved in moving from where you are now to where you want to be in the future may require a series of decisions, made only when you are ready to discover and apply them.

This appears to present a problem, doesn't it? When you're in a crisis, you want out of it *now*, especially if it's a personal crisis affecting your emotions. But your teenage daughter likely didn't begin using drugs the moment you discovered them. The marriage that crumbled through infidelity or incompatibility wasn't perfect up to the day one of you demanded a divorce. And your creditors didn't get together over coffee this morning to unite in taking legal action against you. Crises take time to shape themselves. Unfortunately, they also often take at least a little time to resolve, although some can be resolved faster and more easily than you imagine.

This is the basis for not taking immediate action in a crisis situation, assuming it has nothing to do with roaring fires and charging bulls. It's not your intelligence or your perception that prevents you from taking the best action to emerge from the crisis. It's evolution.

We inherited certain characteristics from Stone Age ancestors who foraged in an environment in which they were both predator and prey. When these people discovered they were playing the latter role, the survivors were those who were highly efficient at taking one of two alternative actions: fight off the predator, or run fast enough to escape the threat. Those who were good at both managed to live long enough to pass their genes down to future generations. Today we possess the same *fight or flight* response when faced with a threat, and it is deeply rooted in our instincts.

Fight or flight works well when the choice is either eat or be eaten, but not so well when the threat is essentially emotional, and that's at the core of most personal crises we encounter. Think of Darren's response to the ATM that gobbled his bank card. He was prepared to battle an unfeeling, unresponsive machine because that was the only response that several thousand generations of ancestors had prepared him to have. Perhaps you would have remained totally cool and worked your way logically through the situation. If so, good for you. This would have been the intellectual response to the problem. Too often, however, in the middle of a personal crisis your intelligence is overwhelmed by your emotions. When neither flight nor fight is appropriate, you are intellectually bereft. You become, in effect, the dumbest person in the room.

We all suffer crises in our lives, but we don't all agree on just what the word means and how the crisis will affect us. When I asked some people for their definition of a crisis, one of the most common responses was *disaster*. Others suggested *danger*, *catastrophe*, *tragedy*, and similar words. But that's not really what *crisis* means according to those who assemble dictionaries, such as the people at Oxford. The core of the word's meaning has nothing to do with emotional pain and distress. Here is how the *Oxford English Dictionary*, still the ultimate arbiter of the English language, defines the word *crisis*:

> *A turning point in the progress of anything; also, a state of affairs in which a decisive change for better or worse is imminent.*

No mention of disaster. No reference to danger or tragedy. Nothing to suggest heartbreak or misfortune. The *Oxford* tells us that crisis means *change*. If you can remember that the crisis you are enduring does not necessarily mean devastation to your life and happiness, you will be better equipped to follow the steps I'll explain, and to deal with your situation.

A crisis is not necessarily an ending, a pause, or a total stop. It is *a turning point*. Something is changing, or about to change. Your control over how things are changing may be limited, but *your reaction to the change is entirely in your hands*. If your reaction is to remain emotionally paralyzed, unable to respond in any manner, you lose control over the path the crisis will follow.

TWO

# Facing Our Fears

*The thinking process that created the situation*
*is not the thinking process that will get us out of it.*
—ALBERT EINSTEIN

If I tried, I'm sure I could sit down and fill a page or two with memories of the personal crises I have faced through my life so far. You could do the same thing. If we put them in order of their seriousness, I suppose mine would be that morning, just a few days before Christmas, when I stood alone on Jarvis Street and realized I would die that way if I didn't change.

The rest of the crises I have encountered over my life were perhaps not as dramatic and unique, but they were important anyway. Many of them were connected to my business dealings. Anyone who has launched a new business, with or without partners, knows the kinds of crises I mean. I've been pleased to be able to provide a very comfortable life for my family, but there

have been times in the past few years when a business decision I
made threatened to wipe out all that comfort and security. It was
only by handling the situation, using the methods I am providing
in this book, that I managed to retain them.

Other crises may seem very small when viewed from the
perspective of passing time, but they were critical when they
occurred, and they needed addressing in the same manner.

The list of crises experienced through your life would be just
as varied and unique as my own. Some you would acknowledge
as being severe—maybe even life-threatening as well as life-
changing. Looking back on others you may ask yourself, "What
the heck got me so upset about *that*?"

I can be fairly certain, however, that neither you nor I have
ever been faced with the kind of crisis a man in Texas named
Michael Morton needed to deal with in his life. One day in 1986
Morton left for work at a grocery store at six in the morning,
leaving his wife and three-year-old son asleep in their home. A
few hours later a neighbor discovered Morton's wife beaten to
death in her bed and their son wailing in fear.

The police, following routine procedure, narrowed their focus
to Morton and soon charged him with first-degree murder. He
was convicted and sentenced to life in prison without parole.

Morton was innocent, and the prosecutor obtained the
conviction by ignoring evidence that might have proved his
innocence. The evidence included a description of the killer by
the little boy who had witnessed it all, a portrayal of a prowler
provided by neighbors, the use of the wife's credit card and a
forged check three days after her murder, and testimony by
Morton's coworkers that his appearance and attitude at work

that morning were totally normal and not the kind you would expect from a man who had just bludgeoned his wife to death. None of it worked.

Morton spent twenty-five years in a federal prison in Texas before DNA evidence not only proved his innocence but identified the actual killer, who had gone on to kill another woman in similar fashion a year or two after murdering Morton's wife.

Can you imagine spending twenty-five years in a maximum-security prison knowing that you were totally innocent and that proof existed to confirm your innocence? How angry would you be?

Yet when Morton was finally released and then swamped with requests for interviews from people such as Katie Couric and shows like *60 Minutes*, he responded by saying he was not angry. "I am at peace," he said whenever the question was asked.

That's a remarkable statement, but it did not surprise me. Because the first rule in dealing with personal crises, or any other challenge thrown at you by life, is to find peace within yourself. Without peace, you are doomed to be controlled by the crisis and by everyone associated with it. Many people saw Morton's story as a tale of injustice, which it most surely is. It is also, however, a lesson on the importance of finding peace, no matter what grievance you have suffered.

Recalling the definition of *crisis* as *a turning point*, you can understand that the future may be markedly different from the past with which you have grown familiar and comfortable. When you are pleased with your life, and something or someone comes along to dramatically change it without your knowledge or approval, fear is likely your deepest and most painful emotion.

That's what happened to an acquaintance of mine I'll call Larry. In the midst of his crisis he considered suicide, which he associated with feelings of depression. At the root of it all, however, was fear.

Larry was in the publishing industry and, on the cusp of his fiftieth birthday, had never been happier. His second marriage, to a woman more than ten years younger, was as fulfilling and satisfying to him as his career. He had recently been awarded the highest recognition in his industry. Friends and business associates congratulated him on his success, and he realized he had achieved almost all of the goals he had dreamed of achieving years earlier. There had been bumps along the way. There usually are. His first marriage had collapsed partly as a result of his own selfishness, although his children appeared to have recovered well. And his debts were higher than he wished, but he was hardly alone in that predicament. These things happen, he told himself, when you aim for the good life and, given a few months or years, they should resolve themselves.

But Larry didn't have time to wipe away those debts as he had expected to. One month to the day after Larry received his industry's top award, his second wife, Frances, announced that she had been having an affair with a man Larry knew slightly, and she would be seeking a divorce.

The irony of being on top of the world and then being swept up in shock, anger, sorrow, and fear exactly one month later was overwhelming to Larry. Everything he had used to mark his success in life to that point—his career, his splendid home, and his ten-year marriage to a "trophy wife" (Frances often described herself this way with a lighthearted laugh)—vanished. Larry would have to sell his company and divide whatever assets he retained in his home with Frances.

A week after Frances moved out, Larry seriously contemplated suicide. A rope suspended from a rafter in the garage, a metal toolbox to step from, a note to leave … why not?

Fortunately he chose to call Tanya, his daughter from his first marriage, just to hear her voice again. At twenty-two years of age his daughter was mature and perceptive. She also loved her father, despite the pain he had caused his family when he left them. They had remained close and, when his daughter recognized the seriousness of Larry's situation, she told him that she loved him and would come to stay with him for a few days.

That was enough to dissuade Larry from stepping off the toolbox with a rope around his neck. His daughter's presence calmed and reassured him, and he began to deal with the situation in a rational if not painless manner. Things needed to be done, and they were. A month later Larry was surprised at how methodically he had dealt with the situation. A year later he had reestablished his business on a smaller scale but without the debt concerns he had been carrying in the past. Three years later he married a woman closer to his age who managed to provide Larry with happiness from a different and more mature direction.

I know Larry personally. We have worked on a couple of projects, and I can confirm that he emerged from what he recalls as the most serious crisis of his life with even greater confidence and success. It's not a feel-good Hollywood ending. It's just a tale of someone who managed to handle the situation despite his fears for the future. In fact, he had no reason to fear the future.

Given time and his ability to do the next right thing in a step-by-step fashion he learned to welcome it.

Something happened to Larry when he chose not to end his life and called his daughter. Your response may be to say, "Sure, he came to his senses," which is the normal way of putting it, but it doesn't deal with the more complex reality.

Larry's reaction to his situation sounds classic, and it is. Men and women in deep relationships that fall apart unexpectedly react the same way to the news as Larry did. They are in shock, they are in pain, they are incapable of dealing with the situation in a rational manner, and they are obsessed with the fact that their happiness has been yanked away from them, never to return.

If you have ever endured the kind of betrayal that seemingly destroyed Larry's happiness, you understand how he was feeling and perhaps even why he contemplated suicide. Larry was in pain, and suicide represents the ultimate means of ending pain. (It has also accurately been described as *a permanent solution to a temporary problem*.) The fact that it ends *everything* becomes secondary when you are in agony.

But what was Larry really suffering from? What was the true cause of his anguish?

A lot of answers can be submitted to that question. You probably have your own. The list likely includes heartbreak, loss, loneliness, betrayal, and isolation, along with perhaps a dozen more descriptions.

These are all valid, but they are also fuzzy in their definitions. Besides, none of them will help Larry deal with his crisis, and none of them address the nature of crises as defined earlier—the one that says a crisis signifies change.

And how would you have assisted Larry in overcoming those diagnoses? The solution to heartbreak is time. Would it have been enough to say to Larry, "In time, you'll get over this"? Probably not. The cure for loneliness and isolation is to find someone else, but in Larry's frame of mind at that moment, would that have been practical advice?

Instead of dwelling on the obvious emotions, I suggest returning to the definition of crisis. The definition turns on the certainty of change. It does not tell whether the change will be for the better or for the worse, nor does it need to. It is enough to recognize that change is indeed going to happen. And for Larry it had already begun to happen. His life had changed, drastically and suddenly. Think about it:

- He is, or is about to become, no longer married.
- All the glory he basked in just a few weeks ago will be wiped away by the humiliation he is feeling.
- The luxury home he occupied will be lost through the division of marital assets.
- He will have a problem holding on to his business, depending on the divorce settlement.
- His idealistic vision of living happily ever after with Frances is no more.

These are parts of his life that are going to change for certain and he doesn't know what will replace them. *He is facing a future he cannot control.*

So here is Larry's situation summed up in one word: fear.

He fears a future that he cannot control and obviously cannot predict.

This appears obvious to you, perhaps, but when either hearing about Larry's ordeal or going through it yourself, would you have described it as fear?

Looking back on my experience of living on the street and focusing each day only on begging enough money to purchase a bottle of wine, I recognize hidden similarities between my situation and Larry's. I was addicted to alcohol. Larry had no similar addiction, but he took as much comfort and security from his situation as I did from the effects of a bottle of cheap wine. Neither of us, before the crisis hit, could seriously imagine giving up the thing we believed we needed to survive. For me it was alcohol. For Larry, it was the comfort he took from the apparent envy of others.

All addictions, including alcohol, are both physical and mental in nature. The physical link is easy to understand when you think of alcohol, drug, and sexual addictions. Many people are surprised to discover the mental factor, but it's true. Withdrawal from any addiction is not just a matter of surviving the body's reluctance to give up whatever it has been dependent on for months or years. It is also a matter of overcoming the mental resistance to the idea.

No one had to tell me that drinking alcohol day after day while ignoring my body's need for nourishment was unhealthy. No one needs to tell a drug addict the same thing. A bottle of wine or three injections of heroin is not a healthy daily diet. That's clear to everyone, including alcoholics and addicts. The solution is obvious to alcoholics and other addicts on an intellectual level but inaccessible at an emotional level. We know what must be done, but we are not equipped on an emotional level to take the steps. Why not? Because we fear what we cannot control and cannot predict.

It's an extension of the old adage: *The devil you know is preferable to the devil you don't know.*

I knew what my life on the street was all about. I knew who my friends were, I knew what my day would consist of, I knew how to get my hands on what I needed to get through the day, and I knew the feeling that a drink of alcohol would provide me.

I did not know what life elsewhere would be like, where I would meet new friends I could trust as much as my street buddies, how I would spend my days away from them, and how I would survive without alcohol. That was the future that faced me when I considered getting off the street, and the prospect frightened the hell out of me.

Until I was able to step away from my fear of the future—my anxiety over changing a life that I knew was empty and doomed—none of the options available to me were within reach. In many ways, that's what this book is about. It is about dealing with your fears of the future—the one dictated by the circumstances of your current crisis—so that you can face reality and do the next right thing.

And here's an eye-opener: You don't need to be in the midst of a serious emotional crisis to be dealing with your fears for the future. Fear is common to all of us, to one extent or another. Each morning when I wake and rise out of bed, I am aware of two emotions, and their levels vary according to whatever is happening in my life at the moment. One is anticipation: What's going to happen today? Will the plans I made yesterday work out well? Will I receive good news that I've been expecting, or (even better) good news that I didn't see coming?

The other emotion is fear, and it is both normal and expected. Everyone fears things not working out, or working out differently from their expectations. We just pretend the fears are not around. You have probably learned to submerge a fear that may be lurking just beyond your door. It can have different labels—stress or tension—but it's still fear, and until you recognize it as such, you won't be capable of dealing with the problems it can cause. Whenever you let this happen, you are prevented from dealing with things in what would be considered a rational and effective manner.

I realized this recently when I met a woman who told me she was concerned about her seventeen-year-old son. His life, in her opinion, was a disaster. "He won't clean his room or make his bed," she said, and as she went on with her story her anguish became more and more apparent. "His schoolwork is terrible, he's not applying himself to his education," she complained. "The way he's going, he'll wind up flipping hamburgers for a living and staying with me for the rest of his life!"

Her son's status was all she could talk about. It appeared to me that she *needed* to have it occupy her thoughts. That's probably not true, of course, but she used this particular concern about her son's future to fill her consciousness, as though she had to have something to worry about.

The challenge for her was to stop thinking in this manner. She needed to accept that her son, somewhere at some time, would encounter a means to influence his life and persuade him to do what he had to do. It would probably be called maturity, and it was certain to arrive at some point in his life. She believed that she needed to change her son, but she was wrong—totally, tragically wrong. Instead of trying to change her son, she needed to stop thinking about the child. That was the next right thing to do—not lying awake at night imagining the worst for the boy, and not buttonholing everyone she met who might have advice to offer. Advice won't change this kid. Something will at the right time, but it won't be words of wisdom from his mother, from me, or from anybody else. Things will work out as they should, and her fear—*your* fear, in your own unique situations—should be bypassed and ignored.

Some may call this approach abdication. I call it an intelligent response.

To put it bluntly, the woman was thinking about nonsense. She needed to stop focusing on unmade beds and future employment prospects and start realizing that life is worthwhile—*her* life. Her overriding concern for her son was not changing him, nor would it ever change him. At seventeen years of age, he was locked in to his behavior patterns where housekeeping and homework were concerned. Whatever his mother could say, whatever she could do, had already been done with no effect. Repeating it over and over again with the expectation that this time it will work, believing that this time the message will get through, is absurd.

I suspect the woman anticipated that I would provide her with some secret strategy for changing her son's behavior, some elixir of wisdom to be applied in measured doses with dramatic results. If so, my words undoubtedly surprised her.

"Stop thinking this way," I advised her. "Find something bigger and more influential than either you or me to deal with your situation, and trust that things will work out. They always have, and they will continue to do so." I assured her that some things would go wrong. When they did, it would be up to her son to make the changes he needed to make. It would be his own crisis to deal with, his own experience of handling *a turning point in the progress of anything*, as the good people of the *Oxford English Dictionary* put it.

You can offer advice and the value of your own experience, but you cannot change someone else's life once that person develops an awareness of free will. Sigmund Freud and all the analysts who have ridden on his shoulders recognized this fact. Yes, an individual can change his or her behavior for the better, rising above various challenges and weaknesses. But only if he or she wants to change. Otherwise, the wisdom of Freud or Einstein or anyone else will flow through his or her mind unabsorbed, like water down a glass mountain. The woman fretting about the future of her teenage son may have been either enlightened or dismayed by my words. I only know that the nature of my advice surprised her, because it wasn't what she expected to hear.

When you're in the midst of a personal crisis, the obvious thing to do is not the first thing that springs to mind. How often have you heard of a friend or relative who, when faced with a crisis in his or her life, made a stunningly foolish decision? "Why would he/she do a thing like that?" you ask yourself. "Doesn't he/she know this will only make things worse?" As a matter of fact, people usually don't know that. Because fear and stress do more than cripple their thought process; they also make them dumb.

Most people are surprised to discover this aspect of stress, the one that inhibits your ability to think with the same skill as before the crisis arrived. Stress makes you dumb? Isn't it supposed to make you courageous? Ernest Hemingway appeared to believe this when he famously defined courage (he called it "guts") as *grace under pressure*. Hemingway was a fine writer and a good judge of character, but he was a little off base on this one. Can you weave your way through a personal crisis with grace? Probably not.

In reality, most people would lose their grace under the pressure of war, meaning they would fail to deal with the situation in a logical manner. You may think of courage as an admirable quality, and it is. But courage often conflicts with logic, which may explain the heroic actions of soldiers in battle. We consider them brave and filled with courage, but after stepping back from the praise of their heroics, their actions often appear unwise when measured against the idea of self-preservation.

I recall watching a TV interview with a young American soldier in Afghanistan. The soldier had rescued four comrades by manning a machine gun mounted on the open back of a gun-truck while it raced across wild terrain directly in front of some Taliban troops. He and a Marine had set out to assist trapped Afghan troops loyal to the U.S. and recover the bodies of four American soldiers. Taliban fighters in the hills on either side of the road directed their fire at him, while the lone soldier stood unprotected on the bed of the gun-truck as it bounced crazily over the road. Amazingly, he and the driver made two trips as bullets whizzed through the air around him and he remained in place, swinging his machine gun back and forth while firing at the enemy. The soldier survived, and everyone who witnessed his actions praised his courage. His actions won him a Medal of Honor, and during the media interviews leading up to the awarding of the Medal of Honor, he was asked if he felt frightened while risking his life.

"No," he replied, "I didn't feel scared because I expected to be shot and killed each time we crossed in front of the Taliban."*

It is not my intention to denigrate the bravery of this young man in any way, but I wondered how he might have felt the day before the battle. How would he have replied had someone asked if it would be a good idea to stand unprotected in the back of a speeding pickup truck while dozens of Taliban warriors tried to pick him off from the surrounding hills? Would he have agreed to do it when his own life wasn't at stake? Most people, including well-trained and dedicated soldiers in war zones, would likely say no, they would not. They would probably describe the idea as "dumb" and suggest it would be better to avoid such an act to survive and fight another day when they could count on inflicting major losses against the enemy. Under the stress of actual battle with comrades in danger, in the knowledge that "somebody has to do something," and with little or no time to think about it carefully, the soldier made a decision that most people would consider more foolish than wise.

---

* The soldier's name is Dakota Meyer, and he was awarded the Medal of Honor by President Barack Obama on September 15, 2011.

Stress changed the soldier. You could argue, from a perfectly clinical perspective, that it made him braver. You could also argue that it made him dumber.

Think about that for a moment. Then think about this: If you were seeking wise counsel to deal with your personal crisis, would you ask the dumbest person in the room for advice? Not very likely. But while you are in the depths of a personal crisis, the dumbest person in the room is almost always yourself, and yet that's who you tend to rely upon for wise guidance. Which is obviously a major mistake.

Crises don't occur exclusively to individuals. They happen to corporations and governments too. Do companies become foolish when placed under stress due to a crisis? The corporations don't, but the individuals making the top decisions can and often do.

No crisis faced by a company doing business in the U.S. in recent years has been as dramatic and wide-ranging as the one that began with the April 2010 explosion of BP's Deepwater Horizon oil well in the Gulf of Mexico. Tony Hayward, the petroleum company's CEO, was obviously under enormous stress when the media reported that as much as 60,000 barrels of crude oil were spilling into the Gulf of Mexico each day. The impact on him became apparent when he chased away photographers and, in response to his handling of the situation, blurted "I'd like my life back," either ignoring or having forgotten about the eleven people killed and seventeen others severely injured in the explosion. Either way, it made Hayward and, by extension, BP appear oblivious to the wider implications, including the deaths of the workers and the economic and environmental impact all along the Gulf coast.

The BP crisis changed a number of things, including the attitude of many Americans to offshore drilling for oil; the financial situation of BP, which spent billions of dollars to correct the situation and its image in the U.S.; and the CEO himself, who was soon without a job.

Corporations don't always handle crises so awkwardly. Sometimes, in recognition of the change that the crisis is about to cause, they assume a key posture in handling the crisis, then move forward to a position that, in the long run, proves better than their original status. (This, by the way, frequently occurs with individuals such as Larry, who realize later that the change they feared actually delivered a better future for them—as we will see.)

When seven people in the Chicago area died of cyanide poisoning linked to Extra-Strength Tylenol capsules in 1982, the CEO of parent company Johnson & Johnson considered the situation carefully. This was clearly a crisis. The image and dominant market position of Tylenol was about to change, and the CEO accepted this. Trusting that the public would see the move as positive, he ordered the recall and destruction of every existing Tylenol product, including all those in production, in the warehouse, and on the shelves of retail stores, even when it became evident that the manufacturer had nothing to do with the poisonings. The action cost the company more than $100 million. Was it worth it? At the time, some people believed it wasn't. Thirty years later, it's clear they were wrong. By trusting consumers to view their actions as the right thing to do, Johnson & Johnson became and remains among the most highly regarded corporations in the U.S., and Tylenol outsells the next biggest-selling brand of over-the-counter pain medication about four to one.

So what happened here? Think about it:

The CEO of BP couldn't handle all the implications of his company's crisis. He just wanted his life back. The CEO handling Tylenol accepted that things were about to change and trusted that his company's concern for safety would eventually pay off; his actions bolstered the brand's image. Each company moved sharply in a different direction.

You may say, with some justification, that your personal crisis has little to do with these kinds of business crises. Perhaps, but both required their CEO to find a special calm place before taking action to deal with the crisis. The Tylenol CEO found his place quickly, made the decision, and took the right action. The BP CEO focused on the cost to him rather than on the cost to the company and to the members of the public suffering as a result of the incident. That's a natural reaction for anyone to have, initially. But it proved disastrous to BP and eventually to the CEO.

In too many instances, we deal with serious crises by having three reactions, sometimes sequentially, sometimes simultaneously:

1. Why me?
2. I'll fix them!
3. Somebody help me …

These are all understandable responses to being sideswiped by a personal crisis. But these responses don't help you solve a crisis. In many ways they prevent you from dealing with it in an effective manner. Here's why:

1. *Why me?* Because despite all that you may have achieved in your life and all that you are capable of achieving in the future, you are still human. Human beings, including yourself, are neither infallible nor protected from forces beyond their control. We all experience crises and disasters of various kinds that we feel, with some justification, we don't deserve. Asking "Why me?" is like asking why you exist. There is either no answer or there are a million answers. Neither is helpful. The most helpful thing you can do is to stop asking "Why me?" Because the only correct answer to that question is "Why not?"

2. *I'll fix them!* A desire for revenge against someone who brought the crisis down on your head may be understandable, but once again it doesn't solve the crisis. In many ways, it can prolong it. You may have legal means to deal with the action that triggered your crisis, and choose to pursue it. If so, don't expect a legal settlement to provide a satisfying solution. Legal settlements often extend over long periods of time and their outcomes can be unpredictable. What's more, most of the damage has probably been inflicted on your ego, and while

your ego is important to you, it has little standing in a court of law.

Of course, "fixing" them in other ways, including giving serious consideration to using violence, involves many things, all of them bad. If you're thinking of retaliating with violence or some other means of inflicting pain, you don't need to fix "them." You need to fix yourself.

3. *Somebody help me!* You have a right to seek help if you believe you need it, and you should consider three sources of assistance. The first is your family and friends, if they are available and not the core of your crisis. Talk to them. Discuss your feelings and fears. Absorb their advice and thank them for it.

Along with (or in place of) the comfort of family and friends, you can turn to professional assistance. If your personal crisis is causing deep and extended feelings of depression, it is crucial that you contact your physician or a counselor immediately. Do it now.

The third and perhaps most important source of help is right at hand. It is the person holding and reading this book.

While I will try to avoid clichés in this book, here is one that I can't sidestep because it is at the core of everything we are dealing with:

*Life is a journey.* The journey varies according to the decisions you make and the kind of life you pursue. To an ascetic monk, life is an uneventful journey from birth to death, a straight line across a flat landscape devoid of distractions that arise from materialism or, in many instances, from sensual pleasure. To a celebrity or a daredevil, life is a chain of exciting events linked by enormous rewards and heart-stopping risks. To most people, the journey consists of an unpredictable blend of smooth cruising, rough sledding, sudden turns, steep hills, new vistas, frustrating detours, and the odd flat tire. In other words, it's a motor trip across the continent accompanied by an out-of-date road map and an often changing cast of companions.

You may prefer to describe your life as a passage, a tour, an excursion, or a stumble across uncharted land. Call it what you will, you are almost always in psychic motion, never at ease. Life involves progress, it involves change, and it involves challenges. The size and impact of each varies by many things, including your age and economic status. Relaxing on your front porch in a creaky rocking chair with a cool drink at hand and a good book to read is wonderful, but it's not life. It's a respite from life. Somewhere, sometime, you have to repair that rocker, mix that drink, finish that book, and eventually get up and do some chores.

Life is motion of one kind or another. Like it or not, you are traveling from womb to tomb. As long as you are alive you are in motion, and when you are in motion things happen in your life just as they happen on any extended journey. You hit bumps in the road, you encounter new views, and you acquire new traveling companions. Sometimes you crash into a barrier set up by someone else, or collide with another vehicle driven by an inattentive motorist.

So when you encounter bumps, crashes, detours, and empty fuel tanks, it's not only foolish to assume that they are happening to you exclusively. It is wrong. They happen to everybody on the road, and everyone, one way or another, is on the same road. It's just that some of us are in different lanes.

Besides, it's not the fact that these incidents occur on your life's journey that you must deal with. It's the way you react to them that tells you whether you have absorbed their lessons.

About two thousand years ago, the Roman emperor Marcus Aurelius wrote one of the most insightful observations about being a human that I have encountered. In the midst of any personal crisis, large or small, try to recall his words:

> *If you are pained by an external thing, it is not the thing itself that disturbs you but your own judgment and reaction to it. And it is in your power to wipe out this judgment and reaction.*

Aurelius may have been unrealistic when he suggested that we all have the power needed to "wipe out" our judgment and reaction. He was, after all, a battle-hardened Roman warrior. Otherwise, I think his idea is right on the money. If your spouse or partner decides the relationship is over ... if you lose your retirement savings in a stock market crash or because of an unscrupulous adviser or as a result of your own foolish decisions ... if your parent or some other loved one is facing a terminal illness ... if any of the other events encountered in your journey suddenly blindsides you, *the pain you feel from the external event is caused by your reaction to it.* In most cases you cannot change the event itself (and it's almost always useless to try), but you can always find a way to change your reaction to it.

Tackling all the elements of a crisis requires both courage and awareness—courage to defeat whatever fears and concerns the crisis brings, and awareness of the means to do so.

As we saw in the case of the U.S. soldier in Afghanistan, courage is sometimes linked with reckless action where physical danger is concerned. That's not a major factor when tackling the fears that envelop you in a personal crisis. It's not immediate action you need to move through your crisis. It's cool courage to view the situation calmly and realistically. The more courage you have, based on your identity and your inner confidence, the more you are able to see the situation with clarity and act accordingly.

In my experience, those who are least equipped to respond with coolness in these situations are men and women who bear emotional scars from childhood. Their scars never fade entirely, and the scars color their ability to deal with stress. The abuse I suffered as a child contributed to my inability to deal with alcoholism for years. I have since learned the role it played, and how to suppress the pain that would continue to affect me if I let it. For years I have referred to the scar as My Dark Passenger. It has been with me through most of my life, but I denied its existence because I was ashamed of it. While I don't need to acknowledge its presence, I know it is always there, although it no longer has the power to hurt me.

A similar presence accompanies many individuals whom I have counseled, drawing from my own experiences. I participate in a group called simply the Men's Project, in which male members share their concerns and experiences with others. It is often a difficult thing for men, especially men "of a certain age," to discuss events in their lives that have caused them great emotional pain. It goes against the grain of our admittedly old-fashioned but deeply entrenched need to conceal our sensitivities and vulnerabilities. It happens within an atmosphere of honesty and trust, however, and listening to these men share stories of their lives and their anxieties, I have been struck by the correlation between the frequency of childhood abuse they suffered and their difficulty as an adult in dealing with personal crises.

Many of these men are highly successful individuals who have achieved leadership positions in their business and professional lives. The scars they carry are easily concealed when they are in control and events are unfolding for them as anticipated. When faced with a challenge to their corporate responsibilities or to some professional difficulty, they have little trouble determining what needs to be done and taking the appropriate action. Only when unexpected and unwelcome change occurs to them personally do the scars on their psyches erupt. That's when they revert, in their fears, to the children they were when the abuses occurred. Physical, emotional, or sexual abuse leaves scars on undeveloped minds, and as much as you work at dulling the pain and suppressing the agony, it remains with you, and you need to acknowledge it.

Still, *you are entitled to your emotional response.* Yes, it's often painful and even destructive to your ego, but you should not apologize for it. You can't deny or attempt to conceal your initial feelings without rejecting your own humanity. We need to accept the right to our emotional response. We need a means of changing our judgment and reaction before moving on, leaving the crisis behind.

That isn't easy. We are all creatures of habit, after all. In fact, one of the reasons for our intense response to crises is that, in our hearts, we recognize the Oxford definition of the word— *a decisive change for better or worse is imminent*—and we are frightened to make the kind of change that will be necessary.

A number of therapists have begun using the term *default* when discussing aspects of personalities. The word was inspired by computer programmers. When you choose not to establish a special task or setting into a program, the computer assumes its default position. You don't have to think about it. When you don't make the decision, the computer makes it for you.

As you mature, you assume default settings for many of the things you do and the reactions you have. Default settings become your responses whenever you are unable or unwilling to take any specific action in the face of a new situation. They're not habits. They're the way you have programmed your life, usually unconsciously, and they are so hidden and so persuasive that you never think about them.

Here's the difference between a habit and a default:

*A habit* is a routine that you follow, such as making your first cup of coffee before reading the morning newspaper, followed by taking a shower. You can and probably do break your habit from time to time, depending on your mood and circumstances. It is not programmed into your existence. It is an action you consciously choose because, for most of us, there is something comforting about following a routine. If the newspaper is late one morning, you change your routine and take your shower on the assumption that the newspaper will arrive while you are drying yourself off. (Actually, the telephone usually rings while you are in the bath or shower, but that's a different problem.)

*A default* is neither a habit nor a routine but part of your personality's DNA. You can't change it as easily as you can change a habit, but you can override it with a system to guide you through the process.

Consider the default settings for these three individuals:

Jean is depressed. This happens often and is triggered by her job, her spouse, her family, or some other external influence. Each time it happens, she heads for the freezer and consumes all the ice cream she finds there. If there is no ice cream she walks to the store and buys some. Preferably chocolate.

Jim is having a difficult time at work. He dislikes his boss and can't relate to his coworkers. In moments of honest reflection, he admits that his boss isn't such a bad guy and his coworkers are fine. It's his work that he hates, and he directs his anger at those around him, who mysteriously seem to enjoy the same work that he dislikes. He also believes no other job exists for someone with his training and education. Each time his dissatisfaction reaches a critical level, Jim stops at a bar after work and orders two, sometimes three drinks. Usually Scotch on the rocks. And wonders why his coworkers seem to avoid him.

Jessie keeps getting dumped by her boyfriends. Whenever it occurs, she withdraws into her room and blames herself. She is too fat or too thin. Her hair is too long or too short. She talks too much or doesn't talk enough. When she gets over her latest broken heart, she will change—her hair, her weight, her wardrobe, her personality. Then she will go out, find a new boyfriend … and get dumped again.

All three of them slide into a default mode when faced with a challenge. Jean's default mode is binge eating, Jim's is drinking alcohol, and Jessie's is blaming herself. As long as they remain in default mode, nothing will change. It's like the computer or cell phone you unpack from the box: Its settings have been put in place by someone else. If you choose to accept them, someone else is deciding how your computer or cell phone will operate. Jean, Jim, and Jessie all permit others to press the buttons, turn the keys, or otherwise kick-start a built-in response to a crisis.

And there is the lesson: If you are not happy with the way your default mode operates, it's your responsibility to locate and use a new one that works for *you*.

Looking back at Jean's, Jim's, and Jessie's situations, you can probably identify the "settings" that each needs to change. Jean needs to stop believing food is a cure for depression and seek professional help. Jim needs to open his mind to looking for work that he finds interesting and fulfilling instead of blinding himself to reality with alcohol. And Jessie needs to avoid blaming herself for her heartaches and begin choosing better boyfriends.

So why don't they try these solutions? Because changing your emotional DNA is almost as difficult as changing your genome code. Besides, Jean's, Jim's, and Jessie's default reactions actually work. For a while. Jean is comforted by the chocolate ice cream, Jim grows mellow with each glass of Scotch he sips, and Jessie believes that all she needs to hold the next man who steals her heart is a new hairstyle or clever repartee.

Each time another difficult situation arises, it's easier to fall back on your default setting than to change your behavior entirely. Yet change is what you need when you encounter a genuine crisis in your life. Remember the *Oxford English Dictionary's* definition of crisis? It means *a turning point*, an opportunity, or a desperate need for change. But change will never happen if you keep doing the same thing over and over.

There is an even larger concern. Let's return to the computer or cell phone analogy. If something occurs in a programmed device that the equipment's default setting cannot handle, what happens? The whole system crashes.

When you face a personal crisis that is beyond the capability of your default settings, you are certain to crash. It may be an emotional breakdown. It may be a series of bad decisions based on the emotional impact of the crisis. It could even lead to an attempt at suicide.

Consider what happened to Larry. His default setting for dealing with other stressful situations grew overloaded with the unexpected departure of his wife. He was fortunate enough to reflect on his actions and back away. Others do not. Each year almost forty thousand people in the U.S. and Canada succeed at taking their own lives.*

---

* Centers for Disease Control and Prevention, National Center for Injury Prevention and Control, Web-based Injury Statistics Query and Reporting System (WISQARS), 2010 (cited 2012 Oct 19).

Statistics Canada. *Suicides and rate of suicide according to sex and age*, Ottawa: Statistics Canada; 2010, www.statcan.gc.ca/tables-tableaux/sumsom/101/cst01/hlth66a-eng.htm (accessed 2012 Nov 13).

Default responses do not work. We need something better. Larry, without knowing it, provided the means for dealing with his crisis and assisting you to deal with yours.

When Larry recalled his daughter, remembered her love for him, and wrapped himself in the serenity of that vision, he found peace. And finding peace is the most important lesson in this book.

# THREE

# All We Do Is Behave

*Our deeds pursue us from afar,*
*And what we have been makes us what we are.*
—JOHN FLETCHER, *THE HONEST MAN'S FORTUNE*, 1613

Our lives are unique, but the crises we face are not unusual. Many of the crises that people encounter through life sound familiar to you because either you or someone you know has experienced them in one form or another. The difference among crises is almost always measured not by what happened to you but by the way you reacted.

All kinds of things affect your reactions—your values, your social standing, the stage of life you are in when the crises occur, and other influences. The same things also affect your response to others whom you see in a crisis. How would you react, for example, to the sight of an unshaved and unwashed man dressed in dingy clothes, thrusting his dirty hands at you and asking if you could spare some change? Whether your response was sympathetic or dismissive, the descriptive words that might lurk at the back of your mind could include *loser, lowlife, poverty-stricken, abandoned, lazy,* and *unloved.*

These are not flattering words, and they shouldn't reflect any prejudice on the part of the person thinking them (although they often do). They are applied in trying to explain the state of someone who is worse off than we are. Yet these words are often wrong.

They would have been wrong applied to me as a young alcoholic in Toronto. I came from a solid middle-class family with active and successful parents—my father was a factory manager—and concerned siblings. I wasn't lazy or abandoned, and whether I realized it or not, I was loved. And one of the men who shared the same street corners with me, asking the same passersby for the same handouts so he could buy a bottle of the same brand of cheap wine, had been a practicing physician. He had completed medical school and launched a successful practice before it all fell apart due to his alcohol addiction. You could call Doc—the only name I knew him by—many things, but not stupid or lazy. Grappling with alcoholism or a similar problem is not a unique crisis. It's how you respond to the crisis that varies, and this may seem to suggest that different people need different ways to handle things.

Well, that's not necessarily the case. One of my goals in writing this book is to demonstrate that although we react differently to crises, we need a common method of working our way through them. And it exists.

Consider a young woman's unwanted pregnancy, for example. From Hollywood movies to the girl down the street in your town, or maybe even to a member of your own family, the tale of a woman faced with the crisis of an unwanted pregnancy that will change her life, no matter what decision she makes, is common and familiar.

I recently heard of a young woman I'll call Jennifer. The core of her story could have been told in a Victorian-era tearjerker. The primary difference between Jennifer's life story and a book such as *Tess of the d'Urbervilles* is the outcome; Tess died as a result of her misfortune, a prospect that Jennifer, for all of her worries, needn't fear.

Living on her own and planning to return to university to complete her degree studies in a year or two, Jennifer became involved with a married man at the office where she worked. She became pregnant. Hearing of her plight, the man expressed sympathy and not much else. He made it clear that he would not leave his wife, and expressed no interest in the child that Jennifer might give birth to. He suggested Jennifer take steps to ensure that she did not give birth to the baby. He would pay any costs associated with an abortion.

The trouble was that Jennifer's parents, who lived about 40 miles away in her hometown, were opposed to abortion. They took part in protest rallies against the practice. They had also poured all of their love and support into her. As I understood it, if Jennifer were to seek an abortion, she would feel for the rest of her life that she had betrayed her parents. If she had the baby, they would surely accept it, but she was neither prepared nor equipped to become a single mother. For a week or more she was paralyzed in fear and sadness. She had to do something. If she did nothing her body would make the decision for her in less than nine months.

I don't have any statistics on the matter, but I suspect that an untold number of young women find themselves in the same plight as Jennifer day after day. Some of them may have no hesitation at all in making the decision they feel is best for them. Most, it seems to me, are not able to deal with things so quickly. And, as we'll see in the next chapter or two, there's a very good reason why.

Let's not minimize Jennifer's crisis just because it's so common. The fact that millions of unwanted and unexpected pregnancies occur each year does not make it less challenging for Jennifer. A million crises happening to others is a statistic. A crisis like Jennifer's happening to her—or to you—is a tragedy.

We may handle a serious crisis in different ways, but our bodies are programmed to react in the same way: by freezing up emotionally. It's buried within our genes. Not being able to reach a decision that appears beneficial, under the circumstances, is part of the fight-or-flight response handed down from our cave-dwelling ancestors.

Fight or flight is the default setting for anyone in an emotional crisis. When you encounter a situation that requires more than the capabilities of this setting, you become emotionally and physically paralyzed. When you can't run away from a fact and there is no one to fight, it's as though your programs have crashed. You become like your computer when it crashes; you freeze up, and for a while at least, no amount of teeth-gnashing or threats can get you to respond. About the only thing you can identify is the need for help, and "help" in this case may mean having someone appear at your side and tell you what to do. Why? Because, assuming you have never encountered this specific crisis in the past, you don't *know* what to do.

The reality is that in the midst of a personal crisis, no one can "tell" you what to do to alleviate the situation. Professional therapists play their role by assisting their patients and clients to overcome the emotional agony first. Then, with the pain under control, people begin to find the means, with their therapists' assistance, of making wise decisions.

My own experience, combined with the experiences people told me about after they either read my first book, *When All You Have Is Hope*, or attended one of my public speaking events, has identified several common responses to crises. I have narrowed them down to five, and they are important to understand because they illustrate the challenges you will face in dealing with personal crises. Whatever your personal crisis may be now or whatever crises you may have faced in the past, I suspect that your responses include most, if not all of these five:

1.  *You feel overwhelmed.* It's too much for you to handle. You feel that you can't deal with the crisis alone, yet you believe there is no one who can either fully appreciate your crisis or provide the means to solve it. This invariably leads to the second point.
2.  *You are all alone.* I've noted that both genders have this feeling in the midst of a crisis for different reasons. Men want to retain the alpha-male identity, able to handle whatever life throws at them.

Women don't wish to burden friends or family with their problems. These are dangerous positions to take. Aside from providing no solution to the problem you're facing, feelings of isolation and the sense that "no one cares" or "no one can help" may have devastating consequences for some people.

3. *You deny reality.* Wishing to hide away somewhere and pretend your crisis isn't really happening is a natural reaction. It's also immature. As an alcoholic, I heard denial day after day. "I'm not an alcoholic," people kept repeating, and one of them was me. "I can stop anytime I want," and "I'll sober up and get a job tomorrow." Only when I came face-to-face with reality and admitted that I would soon die from my addiction unless I found help to overcome it, did I know just what I had to do.

4. *You blame yourself for your situation.* Accepting responsibility is a mature reaction to a crisis, but focusing on what you may have done or failed to do in the past is not helpful in determining what you must do *now*. If you're facing a financial crisis, sitting around thinking, "If only I hadn't spent all that money" won't bring back the money. If you are dealing with a broken relationship, telling yourself "If only I had been nicer to her/him" won't bring back your partner, lover, or spouse, and will only lower your self-esteem even further. Besides, from what I have learned from people whose confidence was shattered by a partner's abandonment, being

"nicer" would not have succeeded in persuading the
other person to stay around. Avoiding self-blame
in the middle of a crisis is difficult, I admit. For one
thing, it makes you feel better, if only because it
identifies the presumed cause. At least (you believe),
now you know why this disaster happened.

5. *You cannot make a rational decision.* No surprise here.
Making a decision means moving forward into
a new space and a new future, and this generates
fear. In other words, it is perfectly rational to be
unable to make a rational decision. Even when you
know it's necessary you will avoid it because, along
with fearing the future, you fear making a wrong
decision. "What if I decide to do *this* when I should
be doing *that?*" is a common state of mind. But as
long as you make no decision, you are failing to deal
with the crisis. And failing to deal with the crisis
means you will continue to suffer from its negative
effects on you. You need to find a place where
not only do you feel comfortable about making a
decision, but also you feel confident that, large or
small, the decision is a good one.

If you cannot make a wise decision based exclusively on your
emotions—and the truth is, you can't—you need to find a logical
means of dealing with your crisis.

This may seem difficult to tackle when your nerves are on fire,
your self-esteem is at a low ebb, and you just want the emotional
pain to go away. Under those conditions, thinking and acting

logically may seem as impossible as flapping your arms and flying.

When trapped in a crisis situation that appears to offer no apparent solution, everyone tends to want the same thing:

*You want somebody to do something. But the only one qualified to do something effectively is you.*

If this includes accepting the fact that you cannot alleviate the pain you are feeling, it is up to you to seek out the help you need, describe your situation, and rely upon the professional counseling you might obtain to assist you through it. You cannot expect the counselors to locate you. And you cannot afford to cling to some pride-based determination to solve everything on your own. Understanding just how serious things are and seeking peace is not a sign of weakness. It is a sign of strength. And perhaps intelligence as well.

The best guidance I know of in this situation comes from two men born more than two thousand years apart, one in Rome and the other in Southern California. The first you have already met: Marcus Aurelius, whom I quoted earlier about being in control of your own responses to a situation if you cannot control the situation yourself. The second is a psychiatrist named William Glasser, who developed an insight into treating human behavior in a new way he called Choice Theory.* Glasser explained that the only behavior we can control is our own, which also explains that all of our most serious psychological problems are rooted in our relationships.

* William Glasser. *Choice Theory: A New Psychology of Personal Freedom* (HarperCollins, 1998).

Think of that in connection with Jennifer's situation. Her primary concern is not about her pregnancy. She is shattered by Benjamin's abandonment and frightened by the thought of her parents' reaction. The status of her pregnancy is not currently an issue. And while she obviously would like Benjamin to maintain their relationship, and desperately needs to find a way of dealing with things that will not destroy her relationship with her parents, she can only do this by controlling their behavior—which she can't do.

Dr. Glasser also notes that everything you do today is related to what you have done in the past, and you can't change that either. The only thing you can truly control is satisfying your emotional needs in the future. Dr. Glasser sums up our situation in life with five simple words that clarify a very basic insight into who we are and how we can learn to deal with personal crises:

*All we do is behave.*

In the case of dealing with the first impact of a personal crisis, we could replace *behave* with *react*. The word *behave*, however, encompasses more of our actions.

Dr. Glasser breaks our behavior into four categories:

1. Acting
2. Thinking
3. Feeling
4. Physiology

Of these four, we have direct control over the first two. We can choose how we act and what we think, but we cannot change how we feel or the way our bodies react to stress, except by changing the first two. If we choose to act and think in a manner that relieves our stress and enables us to deal with the reality we're facing, our feelings will become more positive and our physiology will function normally.

The lesson from this is important, not only for dealing with physical crises but in almost everything you do. If you act and think in the best manner possible given the situation, you will improve your feelings—your emotional well-being—and suppress the negative physiological responses, including loss of appetite, difficulty sleeping, and a range of others. It's a variation on the idea I proposed at the opening of this book, explaining that free will lies in your choice of thought. In other words:

*You are more in control than you realize.*

The natural reaction you have of shock and surprise when faced with a crisis doesn't have to overwhelm you. It's true that you can't avoid your initial response, because it's built into your DNA. But it doesn't have to dominate you either.

Have you ever stubbed your toe while in your slippers or bare feet—say, while walking through your bedroom? I have. It hurt like hell, and my initial response was to shout in pain and direct a few off-color and blasphemous comments toward fate or the gods or whatever it was that caused my momentary agony. When this happened no one heard me except my wife, Nancy, who simply rolled her eyes and continued what she was doing at the time.

I also once stubbed my toe at a church wedding while wearing a very light pair of shoes. The big toe on one foot struck the sharp corner of the pew I was about to enter, exactly at the angle to cause the most discomfort. Was the pain comparable with the time I stubbed my toe in my bedroom? It sure was. Did I howl in pain and demand to know *who the* (insert offensive word here) *was responsible for this insult to my being*? Certainly not. I kept smiling, settled myself in the pew, closed my eyes, and waited for the pain to pass, as I knew it would.

So you can control your reactions according to your environment. When you control your reactions, you control your feelings, and this permits you not only to make decisions but also to make rational decisions. You are no longer the dumbest person in the room.

This is not a variation on the orders insensitive boors give to people in distress, such as, "Snap out of it!" No one "snaps out of" any emotional crisis. Everyone, however, can direct themselves to the point where the crisis is dealt with in a rational manner.

I didn't "snap out of" my addiction to alcohol and the prospect that I would spend my entire life begging for money and sleeping in flophouses. I had to find a place where I could exert as much control as possible over my life and my reactions. Only then was I able to see the reality that I had been ignoring for years and make the wise decision that needed to be made.

This idea of controlling our emotions is easily done on a small scale. It's only when the effects of the crisis are substantial that our feelings overwhelm us.

My idea for this book began with my memories of the day I walked away from a lifestyle that had ground me down, humiliated me, and would almost certainly have killed me one way or another within a few months. What had happened to direct me toward saving my own life? What had made the necessary change possible? What had escaped my drinking buddies, the ones who sought the same refuge in alcohol as I had? Many of them died from that same lifestyle, either as a result of the abuse they subjected their bodies to or of the physical abuse of others who demanded what few possessions they owned.

I survived. I knew how, but I was always uncertain why.

The beginnings of the answer arrived one day some years later when my partner Tom Culligan and I were in the early stages of launching Second Cup. We were pioneering the concept of coffee as a special taste experience during a period when most Canadians and Americans cared only that coffee be dark in color and hot in temperature. It was a revolutionary concept at the time and we were engaged in a learning experience as much as an effort to establish and manage a profitable corporation. Complicating things was a third partner who handled our legal concerns. The man was a good lawyer but a less than outstanding manager, who appeared to see roadblocks to our success with every decision we tried to make. Where he didn't see roadblocks, he created his own, or so it seemed.

Our meetings with this third partner grew more and more frustrating and counterproductive. Every proposal or decision that Tom and I put forward was challenged, and one day I told Tom, "That's it. I'm out of this business. I don't care where it goes. It will no longer matter to me. I am no longer any part of this partnership."

It was not a tantrum, and it wasn't even a crisis on its own, I suppose, but it opened my eyes to a new reality.

I had reached a logically considered decision to deal with an intolerable situation. I no longer wished to pay whatever price was being asked of me. The third partner's involvement in the company had become vexatious and I chose to do without the emotional discomfort he was causing me.

Having made that decision I felt an immediate calmness. I recall thinking, "That was easy." I had no idea what I would do next. It didn't matter. Now that I was free of the emotional burden I had been carrying, I could choose the next step for myself. It was as though I had found something that had been eluding me for a very long time—as though I had been locked in a room, pounding on a door that wouldn't open until I looked around and found a second door that I hadn't known existed. The second door opened and I stepped into sunshine. This was the sensation I recall.

I don't know whether my new, relaxed attitude communicated something to the third partner who had been driving us mad with his antics or whether some other event became influential. I only know that the next day the difficult partner announced to us that he was walking away from the company, that we could have it all to run ourselves without the benefit of his wisdom.

He assumed, I guess, that we would fail miserably without his "wisdom." Instead, Tom Culligan and I built Second Cup into one of the earliest and most successful companies of its kind.

From that point forward, I grew too busy to reflect on what had happened when I chose not to permit myself to be upset again by our partner's antics. But from time to time similar events occurred to reinforce the idea that I might be on to something.

Some years later, long after Second Cup had achieved success and I had sold my share of the company to my partner, I was involved in another major company and dealing with another serious problem. Something had not worked out as I had planned. Despite my efforts and my trust in those around me, the goal I had strived to achieve now seemed beyond my reach, yanked from my grasp by the actions of others, and I had difficulty dealing with it. I was enduring a crisis. Things would change, I knew, and not in the direction I had planned.

I withdrew to the company boardroom and sat at the far end of the table, enveloped in my disappointment. A few minutes later our lawyer, a brilliant man named John Campbell, passed by the boardroom, saw me seated there, and sized up the situation completely. "Frank," he said, "stop being disappointed about being disappointed."

At first I thought John was trying to lift me out of my gloom with a little gibberish. Don't be disappointed about being disappointed? What the heck did that mean?

I sat thinking about it until his advice made sense—a lot of sense.

I was hitting a wall, which was obviously disappointing to me. Then I realized there was a reason for my hitting that wall. John's comment had been a less than subtle instruction for me to turn in another direction—to cease pushing in the direction I was headed and try a new route. I couldn't change the facts, but I could change my reaction to them. In this instance, I changed both my reaction and my direction.

I was involved, after all, in a pioneering business concept dealing with a range of challenges that were all new to me and, in their own way, new to everyone else as well. Had I really expected things to unfold exactly as I pictured them? If so, I was not being realistic. I wasn't even being mature. Things would change—the market, the competition, the clients, even the weather. They would affect the way we planned to grow the business. Why should I be disappointed about the inevitable?

I also began thinking about the kinds of crises we face in our lives, and I realized that some crises are caused by our actions, and some are caused by the actions of others. Psychologists and therapists divide these into *absolute crises* and *conditional crises*. They affect us in different ways, so does this mean we deal with them in different ways? I decided to find out.

Absolute crises have nothing directly to do with your own actions. They happen as a result of the natural passage of life—yours and those of everyone you love or care for. An absolute crisis is usually associated with loss. The loss of your youth, the loss of a job, the loss of a family member: all fall into this category. The common factors among absolute crises are that *they cannot be avoided, and they must be dealt with by you primarily*. Not necessarily you alone—family, friends, and professional counseling are all helpful. But the hands-on work is yours to perform. Absolute crises also lack something: guilt. For all the sorrow they may cause, you should not feel guilty about the role you played in their appearance. They will happen with or without you.

You bear no responsibility for an absolute crisis. People die, accidents occur, the economy changes, and there's little you can do to prevent them from occurring. Unless you played the primary role in initiating the crisis—if, for example, your performance or attitude at work caused your employer to fire you—the crisis you face is universal. Right this minute, millions of people around the world are going through the same kinds of emotional agony, at varying levels of discomfort. This doesn't lessen the pain you feel, but it should persuade you to avoid feeling either guilty or put-upon.

Humans are prone to guilt because we are logical thinkers. We look for reasons why things happen, and when we can't locate one easily, we blame ourselves. Guilt is a universal emotion but it is not a helpful one. We have all done things that we regret and for which we feel guilty. Guilt may be an effective teacher but it is a poor motivator. Feeling guilty makes you less effective at taking charge of your life, because it demeans you. If whatever precipitated your crisis makes you feel guilty, you must bury your guilt before you can deal with the situation.

Here are the kinds of guilt commonly experienced by people who encounter an absolute crisis:

- If I hadn't gone out that night, the accident would never have occurred.
- I should never have let my son/daughter join the team/military. His/her injuries are all my fault.
- Why didn't I tell Mother I loved her the last time I saw her? She died not having heard me say that. How could I be so cold?
- If I had been home when he called me a few days before he committed suicide, I might have been able to talk him out of it.

In the midst of a personal crisis you can usually find something you could have done to prevent the crisis—perhaps. This always becomes apparent after the fact, when the consequences are clear and it's too late to take action.

We are heroes in our minds more than in our deeds, and we would all be enormous successes if we had the gift of prophecy. In fact, we would be perfect! But we have neither the gift nor the perfection. In their place, we have the capacity for guilt.

Guilt can arise in anyone at any time as a result of any event. Recently, I heard of a middle-aged man who died of a heart attack. His death occurred shortly after he had had sex with his wife, who immediately blamed herself. "If I had said no, if I had just avoided it," she said, "he would still be alive!"

Well, maybe. Or he might have died carrying out the garbage, watching an exciting football game, or running to catch a bus. Another thought: Assuming her husband took care of his health with regular physical checkups, shouldn't his physician or cardiologist have warned him against sexual activity? Or how about this: If his wife had repeatedly turned down his efforts to have sex with her, would the tension between them have precipitated the same heart attack he suffered? You can see how endless and unproductive this kind of exercise can become.

Most of us already have too many things to blame ourselves for. We don't need to add the cause of our personal crisis to the list, especially when it's an absolute crisis that afflicts nearly all people.

Actress and singer Kitty Carlisle Hart appeared in motion pictures, onstage in hit musicals, and was a mainstay panellist on television game shows from the 1950s through the 1970s. Each day upon arising, Kitty Carlisle stared at her reflection in a mirror and said aloud, "I forgive you." It doesn't matter what she was forgiving herself for; she remained active and vital throughout her long life. She even appeared in a number of stage productions when she was well into her nineties. She died at age ninety-six, no doubt free of guilt.


Conditional crises are situations you can, or should, claim owner-ship of. The crisis is born within you, not beyond you. It does not occur naturally as an unwelcome byproduct of life. It occurs because you created it and perhaps, without being consciously aware of the fact, encouraged it to thrive. Conditional crises are purely emotional in nature, and our reactions to a condi-tional crisis include fear, guilt (even more than with an absolute crisis, for obvious reasons), anxiety, regret, and other destructive emotions.

Dealing with a conditional crisis is often a mirror image of tackling an absolute crisis. In an absolute crisis you may play no role in its creation but you are the primary and perhaps the only person who can deal directly with its impact. In contrast, you play a major and perhaps the only role in causing a conditional crisis, but you need assistance in dealing with its effects on you.

Jennifer is facing a conditional crisis, although she is hardly responsible for her situation on her own. It does, after all, take two people to cause a pregnancy. The major impact of the crisis, however, will be upon her.

It's clear that Jennifer's lover bears responsibility for her situ-ation, but involving him in dealing with her crisis is a complex issue. While it raises a number of important moral and legal questions, they are not part of her dilemma. Whatever his involvement from this point forward, it will have little effect on the question of Jennifer either choosing to have the baby or seeking an abortion.

A price will be paid for either action. She will either derail her career plans for a time, or she will risk alienating her parents.

One of the biggest lessons you may learn from a crisis is your own vulnerability. Larry was on top of the world emotionally when he won the industry award. He reveled in the support that his wife appeared to show him and it was probably genuine, whatever her state of mind regarding their marriage. Jennifer was young, attractive, and successful in her studies. Neither doubted that his or her happiness would be destroyed with one devastating blow—Larry when told that his wife was leaving him, and Jennifer when she faced a decision that appeared to promise only loss.

You need to accept and understand your own vulnerability even while you are in the midst of a crisis situation that is causing you great pain and uncertainty. You are vulnerable to this pain not just because you are human but because you are sensitive to and respect the feelings of others. In some measures, your own vulnerability represents the best aspect of the human condition.

Time and again, my work with social groups reveals new examples of people solving their problems not by taking immediate action according to their instincts, but by avoiding doing anything until their emotional response fades away and their native intelligence slides back into place. In other words, when they are no longer the dumbest person in the room.

Usually this is the result of suddenly realizing that they need the time, the space, and the inspiration to find the peace they need before attempting to make rational decisions. When this happens, the result is often the same—the crisis is passed, the corner is turned, fear of the future dissolves, and life is rewarding once again.

That's what happened to a man I'll call Mel, whom I encountered in the Men's Project group I mentioned earlier. Mel became a member of the support group as a means of complying with the terms of his probation. He had been convicted of threatening his wife, Alicia, and of creating a general disturbance by virtually destroying their apartment during a violent quarrel. While he had not physically abused Alicia, the court was concerned enough about the prospects to order Mel not to approach his wife during his six-month probationary period. He could contact her by telephone if she approved. If his wife voiced any objection to Mel's calls, they would have to cease until his probation ended. He was also ordered to take anger management classes, and he had joined our Men's Project group on the advice of his probation officer. "It will be more evidence that you're intent on reforming yourself," the officer had told him.

The court decision had devastated Mel. In the first few group sessions, we learned Mel had been abused as an adolescent, which explained but did not excuse his actions. He desperately needed his wife's affection. "I thought my life had ended," he said when he was informed of the court's order to avoid any physical contact with her for six months. "She means that much to me."

Mel attended every weekly meeting of our group, and at each session he brought the other members up to date on his efforts to win back Alicia. She raised no objections to his telephone calls, and Mel tried to be on his best behavior when speaking with her. It became apparent to me and the other members that holding on to his job, living up to the terms of his probation, and recapturing his wife's trust and affection represented the three primary goals of his life.

Whenever he told us about his efforts to reunite with Alicia and her response to them, his emotional attitude revealed everything. Sometimes he would arrive at our meetings smiling from ear to ear. "I made Alicia laugh over the phone the other day," he would say. "I used to make her laugh all the time. She told me that's what attracted her to me. I must have had her laughing on the telephone for an hour!" We would all be pleased for him and then move on to other topics.

At other times, the tears would begin to flow when he mentioned his last contact with Alicia. "I think she may be seeing some other guy," he would almost sob. "She says he's just a friend, but ..." Or he would beg us for advice on what he might do to ensure that Alicia would welcome him back when his probation period was finally over.

Each of us formed our own opinion of Alicia. Most could understand why she was cautious about Mel's promise to respect her if she took him back. Others wondered if Alicia wasn't being somewhat manipulative, perhaps teasing Mel by revealing her involvement with another man one week, and the following week encouraging him to believe she would be ready to welcome him at the end of his probation.

Other things seemed to be happening in Mel's life, good things. Over the weeks we encountered him, each of us recognized a clear and sincere change in Mel's attitude. He became, to put it simply, a nicer guy. Aside from telling us of his attempts to win back Alicia, he was warm, easygoing and fun to be around.

As the end of his six-month probation approached, we began expressing concern among ourselves, out of Mel's earshot, about what might happen if Alicia rejected him. "What if, after six months of toeing the line and trying to be Mr. Wonderful to her, she tells him to get lost when he shows up on her doorstep?" someone asked. "He could crash into a depression that might take a long time to overcome."

"Or," someone else suggested, "he could revert to being as violent as he was when he got into this in the first place."

Two months before the probation period expired, Mel arrived at the meeting looking glum, and when we began our round-table discussion we turned to him first.

"I got papers," he said. "From Alicia's lawyer. She's divorcing me."

There was a sharp intake of breath from everyone at the table. Then we all looked more closely. Mel was sad and concerned but we saw no tears and sensed no repressed anger. Instead, he shrugged his shoulders. "So I guess that's it," he said, and after he had assured us that he didn't need to talk about it anymore, we moved on to other topics.

The following week Mel arrived at the session looking

DO THE NEXT RIGHT THING

relaxed although still a little withdrawn, and the week after he was the same.

At the third meeting after he'd announced his wife's divorce action against him, an entirely new Mel appeared. This one was smiling as soon as he entered the room. He joked with everyone, and when we started our round-table session, he pulled a photograph from his pocket and passed it around. All of us admired the picture of a smiling, attractive woman. "I've got a girlfriend," he said. "She is really nice and we're going to move in together. She makes me happy." He didn't need to tell us. We had figured it out for ourselves.

At the end of his probation Mel dropped out of the Men's Project. One of the members sees him from time to time and reports that he appears happy and, as far as can be told, remains in a relationship with the same woman.


It would be foolish of me to say for certain that Mel has changed his life totally, and that the attitudes that destroyed his relationship with Alicia are all in the past. But I believe it to be true because I have witnessed similar changes in other people who emerged from a crisis situation. The important point to be learned here is that Mel's focus had been fixed on bringing Alicia back into his life. Nothing was permitted to alter his view, his actions, or his thoughts.

The divorce papers changed everything. While some of us in the Men's Project were concerned that this might trigger a violent reaction, as soon as I saw Mel's expression when he told us the news, I realized this was unlikely to occur. *It changes his focus,* I thought. *He couldn't change it himself and now he realizes that someone else has changed it for him. He is looking beyond the collapse of his relationship and his reaction to it. His vision is wider. He will be able to move on.* And apparently he did.

You can change some things in your life, and you cannot change other things. You cannot change the way you behaved in the past, or the way others behaved before you. You cannot change your race, your cultural heritage, or a range of other things that define you. Like the woman who feared her seventeen-year-old son would amount to nothing but a burden for her and society, you should not attempt to change the actions and attitudes of others. But you can change the way you think.

This is your most powerful means of dealing with every crisis you encounter. If you can change the way you think, you can see the crisis from a new angle, one that reveals all of its impact and, from time to time, a new opportunity. To paraphrase one of the most profound ideas of Marcus Aurelius:

> *We cannot change the things that others do to us, but we can change the way we react to them. We can change our way of seeing them. We can change the way we think.*

So where are we now?

We are back to your crises and mine. In my case, I am back to shivering on a Toronto street corner many years ago, feeling something within me change. I am also back to deciding that I will walk away from my plans to help manage Second Cup and build it into a successful nationwide corporation. I am back sitting in the boardroom feeling disappointed.

In the first two examples, I initiated the change on my own. In the third example my friend John offered the strange (at the time) suggestion that I should not feel disappointed about being disappointed; when I heeded his words, things began to change and the universe began unfolding as it should.

What happened? To put it in its simplest terms, *I found peace.*

Having found peace, I stepped beyond the limitations imposed by my emotions. My emotions—my anger, my fears, my disappointments—had all blocked my intellectual abilities to deal with the crises I faced at the time. By neutralizing my emotions through the peace I had located, I was no longer the dumbest person in the room.

First, I found peace.

Then I did the next right thing.

And that's the basis behind dealing with your personal crises.

Simple? It's almost disarmingly simple. The application is a little more complex and the questions you may be asking yourself right now are certainly more numerous. So let's deal with them in detail through the rest of the book.

# FOUR

# First Find Peace

*Life is not just being alive, but being well.*
—MARTIAL, 66 C.E.

People who know me, either through business, friendship, or hearing me speak or read from my book, are surprised when I tell them I wake every morning at five A.M. in a state of fear. Not mind-numbing world-ending deer-in-the-headlights fear. Just the feeling that I will have to face things during the day that I would prefer not to handle, and concern about whether I will handle them correctly. Or at least as best as I can.

We all worry about what each day will hold for us, but most of us conceal it under a layer of anticipation. Hey, it's a new day, with new opportunities, and all of that. That's a lovely attitude, but it's not always one that we can cling to from breakfast to bedtime.

Here is what I have learned to do:

I tackle whatever concerns I have at five in the morning during the first twenty minutes of the day, and dispense with them. In those twenty minutes I look for and find peace, and finding peace carries me through whatever worries I already have and those that I may acquire the rest of the day. Call those first twenty minutes meditation or cleansing or whatever you wish. I call it silencing the noise in my mind, and it is essential to my well-being.

Sometimes most of the twenty-minute period is filled with the same mind-racket I heard when I woke up. What will I do about that? What will she do about this? How will he handle the other thing? Worries, fears, concerns—some of them little more than passing nuisances and some linked to potential serious crises. It doesn't matter. They all occupy my thoughts and they all deserve my attention. But at some point the noise fades into silence, the fears shrink into correct perspective, my mind grows empty, and I am at peace. When I am at peace I always know the next right thing to do. Always.

Does this mean I rise from my twenty minutes of mind relaxation with every decision of my day spread out before me like a smorgasbord of perfect solutions? Not a chance. Life isn't like that and neither is my approach to dealing with crises. It is not necessary to make perfect decisions on every challenge of life you encounter. More than that, it is not realistic. It is simply enough to move the yardstick closer to your goal each day.

Nothing you do in life works at its ultimate level each time you attempt it. Football players don't score touchdowns on every play, dancers don't perform perfect pirouettes in every performance, farmers don't plant bumper crops every spring, and writers don't win literary prizes with every book. Whatever concern you may be facing now or in the future will not likely be solved with a snap of your fingers and a cry of "Eureka!" It's like the children's riddle: How do you eat a whole elephant? One bite at a time.

Look at progress as incremental, something to be achieved through a series of steps, all directed toward the goal you need to reach. And if by chance, or with exceedingly good skill, you resolve a major crisis situation with one quick and clean decision, congratulate yourself (smaller crises are easier to handle; if a major crisis requires an appendectomy, a smaller crisis is like a sliver in your finger). But don't expect to motor through life with the same degree of success.

It's not necessary for me to address any specific problem in those twenty minutes of calm that begin each day, and it shouldn't be for you either. Many mornings, my mind is spinning like a hamster wheel, going around and around and making about as much real progress as the little furry creature that's doing all the running. When the wheel stops turning, things settle down, and the world becomes more clear.

It may take more time than you expect for the hamster to stop running. Some days I have spent almost my entire allotted twenty minutes waiting for the noise in my head to cease, and only in the last two minutes or so have I achieved what I set out to accomplish. Two minutes—that's all. The duration is not important. Only the outcome matters.

When discussing how to deal with personal crises, I refer to finding peace because it's an easy concept to grasp. A more precise word, perhaps, might be *serenity*. When you are serene, you do not feel fear. Instead, you are tranquil and cheerful. Finding your way to that place in the midst of a crisis sounds impossible, but it isn't. It is, however, necessary if you are to deal with the situation by making wise decisions.

The goal is to be serene within your crisis, to deflect the reality that is disturbing your peace and creating your fears with other realities that are positive and encouraging. There is, after all, no magic wand to be waved and no incantation to be employed in handling the challenges we face. Life is not a Harry Potter novel. You will often need to move from a state of fear, anger, disillusionment, and intellectual immobility to serenity in a series of small steps rather than in one great leap.

This may appear difficult at the outset because we are often in pain, and we naturally want fast relief from the agony we're feeling. Relief is always in sight, but it may not be immediately at hand. Moreover, it rarely if ever flies in through the window. It insists that you set out to find it.

Sometimes I take this literally. I go for a walk. If it's a walk through my neighborhood or in a nearby park, I intentionally follow a street or a path I haven't taken before.

"This is too easy!" I hear some readers say. "I'm in agony or drowning in indecision, and O'Dea suggests I *go for a walk*??!!"

Exactly. Sit in a darkened room all you want and you will remain clothed not only in darkness but in despair. Your mind remains a hamster wheel, spinning without making progress. Put your body in motion and your thoughts begin to move as well, away from the closed view and into a more open outlook. Will you discover a solution to your crisis by going for a walk? It's possible, but don't count on it. Instead, count on this: You will be taking the first step toward serenity. Yes, it's a small step perhaps. But it will lead to other steps, all in the right direction.

Whether you walk, ride, or insist on remaining still, you need to focus on finding an answer to this question:

*What can I do right now?*

Not tonight or tomorrow or sometime when you feel better about the crisis you're facing. You need something to do now—this moment, this hour. Preferably it should be more than a decision such as "I can stop thinking about the problem and start thinking nice thoughts." Ideally it should require physical action that represents a step taken, not a decision that can be made and rescinded. Call a friend, consult a lawyer, make travel plans, write a résumé, plant a tree, paint a wall. Determine what you need to do right now, and the need does not have to be directly linked to the cause of your crisis. In fact, it should not be a major decision at all. Not until you find peace. It can be something that simply makes you feel better about yourself and your predicament. The most important measure is not what or where or how or with whom. It is *When?* And the answer is *Right now.*

When it is done, you locate the next step, which is easier to find and even easier to take. And so it goes.

Finding serenity is relatively simple for me because I have been practicing for most of my adult life. As I mentioned, it doesn't always arrive as easily or as quickly as I might like. Sometimes it feels as though there's a traffic jam in my brain, with much horn honking and frustration. But all traffic jams clear up eventually. Things loosen and begin moving. The noises end, the frustration dissolves, and step by step, one by one, the way ahead grows clear. Here's the process:

1.  *Stop.* Stop wondering what to do next. Stop rolling the implications of the crisis around in your mind. Most especially, stop worrying about the future for a moment. Suppress your fears and focus on other things.

2.  *Trust.* There are means of dealing with your crisis. You may have the means yourself. If you haven't, others possess the means. You may believe you are alone, but you are not. You may be required to reach out to others, and you can and must do it. You are searching for strength—others have it and will offer it to you. Having reached out and found a source of strength, trust it to assist you.

3.  *Treasure.* Grasp the things in your life that you value and that give you comfort. If you are loved, if you have a secure place to live and food to eat, if you have friends who care for you, if your health is gener- ally good, if you have a skill or talent that sets you apart—any combination of these qualities is suffi- cient. Consider them and cherish them as a means of taking the first steps toward peace and serenity.

On their own, these three qualities may not be sufficient to deliver the peace you need. But I can assure you that they will reveal the next right thing for you to do. And the next right thing leads you to another stage, bringing you closer to the solution that is waiting for you to encounter it.

I couldn't help thinking about the concept of clearing a traffic jam in my mind when a friend told me about a woman he knows named Tammy. Tammy, he said, was by almost every measure an admirable person. She had faced various challenges in life, and emerged from them stronger and mostly unscathed. Her sense of humor, intelligence, and determination helped her, but these appeared inadequate when she encountered what amounted to a train wreck of problems that threatened her sanity and maybe her existence.

At age forty, Tammy had dealt with a failed marriage, leaving her with an eight-year-old daughter, Emma, and the usual challenges of being a single parent. She handled them well. She found a comfortable apartment, relocated her daughter to a new school, and resumed her training to qualify as a librarian, a goal she had abandoned when pregnant with her daughter. Tammy also maintained a good rapport with her older sister, who lived an hour's drive away and helped Tammy care for their mother, who lived in a retirement residence. She also had a group of friends from her college days who held potluck dinners every few weeks. All in all, she had a social life, a satisfying profession, and a teenage daughter who appeared to be blossoming into a beautiful young woman.

But six years after her divorce everything seemed to collapse. It began when Mark, her boyfriend of two years, chose to end their relationship. He had other plans and other interests, he told her. Okay, these things happen: Tammy refused to wallow in her sorrow like a brokenhearted adolescent, and instead buried herself in her work and her responsibilities as a single parent.

Within two weeks of Mark's departure, the city announced that her library would be closing at the end of the year due to budget cuts, and with little seniority she would likely lose her job. Losing her boyfriend and losing her job were devastating, but that was only the beginning. Barely a week later Tammy discovered a small bag of marijuana in Emma's coat. She barely had time to fret over that one, though, because a neighbor informed her about rumors that the apartment building's owner planned to convert their building to condominiums. When everyone's one-year lease expired, the neighbor said, residents would be asked if they wanted to purchase their apartments for several hundred thousand dollars. If they did not, they would be handed notices to vacate.

Even if her job had been safe, Tammy couldn't afford to buy a condo. Now it sounded as though she had to find a new job by the end of the year, deal with her daughter's use of marijuana, track down the story about the condominium conversion, perhaps find a new place to live, and try somewhere along the way to resurrect her social life. On top of everything else, she felt guilty because, as she told my friend, "I should have seen this coming. I should have had better plans in case I lost my job, and maybe if I had meant more to Mark and been a better mother to Emma, I wouldn't have had to worry about them and could concentrate on my other problems."

What Tammy needed right now, she believed, was a chance to step back from her life and deal with the crises one by one. Then, she was sure, she would return to the relative state of happiness and contentment that she had enjoyed before all these challenges arrived. She would have the peace she felt she deserved. And she was correct. We all deserve peace in our lives. Unfortunately, Tammy had her priorities backward.

Tammy, I suspect, was neither a weakling nor a crybaby. She had taken various blows during her life in stride and found ways to deal with them. She had also taken joy in the good things that life had handed her, including her job, her relationships with her sister and mother, and the achievements of her daughter, Emma, who, up until now at least, had been a straight-A student, captain of her soccer team, and a popular girl with many friends.

Tammy found herself in emotional overload. Her mind was flooded with the traffic jam I mentioned earlier. Each event in her crisis was surmountable on its own if treated as an individual problem. Arriving in tight sequence as they had, the sum of their impact was overwhelming. She needed to isolate each problem and then solve them one by one, without letting other problems distract her from the one she was working on. This seems like the logical way of approaching the crisis. But, as we have seen with others whose emotional response has overwhelmed their intellectual abilities, logic is not always at hand.

As complex and apparently unsolvable as Tammy's crisis may appear, it is something of a classic example. Remember Larry and Jennifer? He was too wrapped up in his own interests to foresee his marriage ending, and Jennifer, for whatever reason, failed to address the risk of pregnancy during her relationship with the child's father. Larry's and Jennifer's crises landed like a ton of bricks on each of them. Tammy's arrived one brick at a time, but the results were similar: an overwhelming weight on her psyche accompanied by failure, disaster, and loss, blended with fear and a small helping of guilt.

It does not matter if your personal crisis resembles those of Larry, Jennifer, or Tammy, or if it is unique to you. You need a means of finding your way back to the world that appeared comfortable and secure before the crisis arrived. You need to halt the free-fall nature of your experience, either anticipating or fearing (likely both) your landing. And you need a way to restore your confidence in a manner that helps you adjust to a new chapter in your life.

The first thing that struck me about Tammy's situation was her strength. On her own she had fashioned a career, held a responsible position, done a good job of parenting her daughter, and established what she assumed to be a permanent relationship.

Sometimes, as in Tammy's case, it appears as though life has conspired to destroy you, or at least test you to the limits of your ability to deal with it. It's not true, of course. In fact, had each of her disasters arrived six months apart it is likely that Tammy would have dealt with them in relative calm, given the strength she had shown in the past.

Consider the crises one by one and how Tammy or you or I might handle them as they landed in our laps:

- *Her boyfriend, Mark, ends their two-year relationship.* Disappointment, heartbreak, loneliness. But

Tammy is not a teenager and this is no high school romance. There are ways of handling the end of a relationship and Tammy, given her independence and intelligence, could find a way of dealing with it through the support of friends and family. She should not assume that she contributed more than Mark to the failure of their relationship.

In fact, she must not feel guilt over any of these events. Guilt is an unproductive emotion; it achieves nothing except to prove you have a conscience. But even your conscience can be mistaken from time to time.

- *Her library is closing at the end of the year.* She will need a new job and perhaps even a new career. She has several months to make the adjustment and perhaps find a more fulfilling and permanent career to pursue.

- *She discovers her daughter is using marijuana.* Serious? Perhaps. Unusual? Hardly. Support groups and guidance in dealing with adolescents and narcotics are widely available. Participating in a group may prove effective at helping Tammy deal with the situation.

- *Her apartment building is about to be converted to condominiums.* Or is it? And when? The news may strike fear in the hearts of many apartment tenants, but this isn't news—it's a rumor. Either the neighbor or Tammy or both may be exaggerating the possibility of this being true. Even if it is true, the process

of converting an apartment building filled with
tenants into a condominium is not easy for the
owners, and various laws, at all levels, exist to protect
tenant rights. This is not a crisis Tammy need worry
about at the moment. In fact, it may not evolve into
a serious crisis at all.

By stepping back from her situation, Tammy may realize
that her biggest challenge is to defeat the feeling of being
overwhelmed. This response can occur to anyone in any given
situation, whether you face an enormous single crisis or a series
of smaller situations or even an apparent minor decision that
suddenly appears insoluble.

So here are three observations that apply to Tammy's crises.
All three represent the basis of my means of dealing with a
personal crisis and the very reason for writing this book:

1. *Her approach to dealing with these crises is backward.*
   Tammy believes she needs to work her way through
   them in order to find the peace she enjoyed before
   this maelstrom of disasters arrived. No, she does
   not. *She must first find peace within herself.* Then she
   can deal with the crises.

2. *There is value in procrastination.* We are almost
   constantly nagged about procrastinating. It sounds
   nonproductive, and it is when you know what you
   need to do and are in the right place to get it done,
   but refuse to do it. When you have neither of these
   qualities at hand, you need time to reflect and

perhaps wait for events to develop before acting.

3. *When you reach the end of your rope … let go.* Enough said.

Tammy finds herself in the middle of a storm—which happens to be an ideal word to describe her situation. You don't create storms. You don't control storms. And you don't welcome their destruction. You need to wait them out, assess the damage, and take steps to restore your life after the storm has passed. Unlike during real storms, in the middle of your crisis you can go on those long walks I spoke of earlier, searching for and finding the small steps you can take as you wait for the storm to pass— and perhaps even help it along.

Each step must be valued not only for the way it takes you closer to the peace and serenity you need, but for the calmness it delivers, and for the way it enables you to think clearly, logically, and intelligently.

Remember that your ability to deal with a crisis situation through logic and intelligence is severely reduced when you are emotionally upset. It is not only difficult to make rational decisions in that situation; it is impossible. Your mind and body have been geared by evolution to save you from a crisis by either fleeing for your life or standing your ground to fight your tormentor. Both responses demand action. Neither calls for intelligence and logic. So how can you take immediate rational action? You can't.

Attached to this realization is a concept that many will either find difficult to consider or reject out of hand. Others will embrace the idea with enthusiasm and gratitude. Here it is:

*The most important step you can take to deal with a major crisis is to trust a Higher Power to bring you peace. In the embrace of feeling peaceful, you will recognize the next right thing to do.*

It is not my intention to debate and promote the existence and nature of God on these pages. Other people with better qualifi-cations have addressed this question and none, to my knowledge, has achieved total success. It is important, however, that you seek, find, and employ your own concept of a Higher Power as a means of handling your crisis by first finding peace.

The best way to obtain inner peace is to bundle all the ques-tions and cares that concern you—the source of all your fears for the future—and hand the package to someone else to solve. This has been, in my view, the premise of all spiritual belief down through the ages. "It's in God's hands now" has been, at its heart, a source of solace. Many phrases you use in everyday life, regard-less of your religious beliefs, reflect this concept of handing off your concerns to someone or something, and no longer being either vexed by or responsible for them. Even if you refuse to admit the existence of this Higher Power that I have been calling God, you desire it.

You desire it because you understand that the growth of the soul leads naturally to inner peace and serenity. By definition, an immature soul resides in an immature person, and immature people are subject to a vast range of fears and uncertainties. Think of the young child frightened by the sound of a thunderstorm, or by the imagined presence of a monster beneath her bed. You may age in physical terms but if your soul remains immature you will never achieve the serenity you seek. You will simply grow fearful of different things.

Once you move from a position of self-will to one that acknowledges the will of a Higher Power, peace is at hand. You become immediately capable of reducing your fears of an unknowable future. But first, of course, you need to acknowledge this Higher Power.

A number of people have experienced the presence of a Higher Power despite their own skepticism. This sensing of the Higher Power's existence and its concern for our well-being has been documented by various people whose belief structures extend over a range of doubts and suspicion.

In a widely praised book published in 2009,* author John Geiger relates several accounts of people who, on the verge of death, encountered an unseen presence that encouraged them to make one final effort to survive. Geiger is hardly a man given to simple-minded mystical fables. Editorial board editor at the *Globe and Mail*, he also serves as president of the Royal Canadian Geographical Society and is a fellow of the Explorers Club of New York. This is a man rooted in down-to-earth reality, not ecclesiastical parables.

Yet he writes with conviction about men and women ranging from members of the 1914 Shackleton South Pole expedition to

---

* John Geiger. *The Third Man Factor: The Secret to Survival in Extreme Environments* (Penguin Canada, 2009).

survivors of the 2001 attacks on the World Trade Center in New York, all describing the apparent presence of a Higher Power—the *third man*—in guiding and encouraging them to find the strength they needed to survive. They include a woman diver lost in a cave more than thirty yards beneath the surface of the ocean, who groped frantically in the darkness with the air in her tanks running out until a voice directed her to the opening. Geiger tells of climbers of Everest and other massive peaks who, finding themselves on the brink of death, become aware of a voice, an individual, a *presence* that persuaded them to avoid catastrophe and survive.

The stories, while individual in their location and threat, are remarkably alike in the recollections of the survivors. Like these two.

The first is from Harry Stoker, a sailor in the Royal Navy who, with two other escaped prisoners of war, was being pursued by Turkish soldiers in the First World War:

> *In the midst of night, I felt—not suddenly or surprisingly—that we were not three men struggling along in line, but four. There was a fourth man, following at the end of our line, in the correct position for a fourth man to be. When we stopped for a few moments' rest he did not join us but remained in the darkness, out of sight; yet as soon as we rose and resumed our march he dropped into his place forthwith. He never spoke, nor did he go ahead to lead us; his attitude seemed just that of the true and loyal friend who says: "I cannot help,*

*but when danger is at hand remember always that*
*I am here to stand—or fall—with you."** 

The second was recorded by a participant in a series of experiments conducted at Laurentian University in 1988 as reported in the *International Journal of Neuroscience*, hardly a publication given to wild flights of religious zeal or hysterical fantasy:

*I felt a presence behind me and along the left side. When I*
*tried to focus on its position, the presence moved. Each time*
*I tried to sense where it was, it moved around. When it*
*moved to the right side, I experienced a deep sense of security*
*like I had not experienced before. I started to cry when I felt*
*it slowly fade away.*†

Geiger suggests an explanation for these and the dozens of other similar events he details in his book. As human beings, we may have acquired what Geiger refers to as an *angel switch* in our genetic makeup, a part of our being that kicks in at times of extreme stress and encourages us not to abandon life and the hope of survival.

Even if the presence of an angel switch is true, it may explain how such a process works but it fails to explain why.

---

* John Geiger. *The Third Man Factor: The Secret to Survival in Extreme Environments* (Penguin Canada, 2009), pp. 60–61.

† John Geiger. *The Third Man Factor: The Secret to Survival in Extreme Environments* (Penguin Canada, 2009), p. 169.

And whatever the answer to that question, the fact remains that too many people to be ignored have undergone a religious or mystical experience that literally saved their lives. The fact that a remarkable number of them were agnostics or atheists makes the situation even more persuasive and leads Geiger to surmise, in the last four words of his book: "We are not alone."

You needn't visualize or justify your perception or rejection of a Higher Power, because it is not necessary to define "Higher Power" any further than to say it is greater than you and is both loving and caring. Accepting this definition means you can include a vast range of identities according to your own needs.

If you need a more specific definition of a Higher Power you can find it in a variety of places. Nature may be one. Your consciousness and existential freedom may be another. You even may find your connection with a Higher Power in science.

I have a deep understanding of the challenge that many people face both in identifying a Higher Power and in accepting its ability to assist them. It is not an unfamiliar problem to me.

As I detailed in *When All You Have Is Hope,* I was sexually abused by two different Catholic priests during my adolescent years. While I refuse to blame them entirely for the downward spiral that took me literally to the gutter, the emotional impact of their attacks was as painful to me as you might imagine. What's more, recent revelations of similar abuses within the Catholic Church confirm that my experience was hardly unique. We will never know how many priests, representing the power and purity of the Church, abused an equally unknown number of children, who represented only trust and innocence. When I desperately needed assistance to help me out of the hopeless trap of alcoholism, where was the Higher Power? Where was the legendary hand of God reaching down to me, there in the gutter, asking me to grip it while it lifted me out of the morass of my desperation? It wasn't there.

I have no difficulty separating the men who abused me from the principles and the religion they were supposed to represent. If the Church can be considered a body, a corpus, these men were the dirt under the body's fingernails and nothing more. The body itself remains as vital to me as ever.

While in the midst of a personal crisis I do not expect that the hand of God or any portion of His being will descend from heaven as a physical presence, welcoming me into the warmth and safety of His palm. I choose to believe the hand exists, but when it reaches out, it reaches through my soul, not through the clouds.

Because of the abuse I suffered at the hands of the priests, and because of other aspects of my life as an adolescent, I rejected the concept of a Higher Power for a time. I grew intent on doing things my way and my way alone, and this led me to my life on skid row. I rose out of that disaster only by placing my life in the hands of a group of people who understood what I had been going through, how difficult it would be to raise myself out of that life alone, and the assistance I would need from them. They were to me a Higher Power, and their care and good works slowly evolved over the years into the Higher Power I now call God.

You may choose to find this power wherever you search, and you may choose to name it whatever you wish. But it exists for all of us, and in the midst of a serious crisis of any kind, we need to trust this power to lead us to a quiet place when the world around us appears to be falling apart.

None of this, I suspect, will make much impact on those who either actively choose to deny the existence of a Higher Power or who intellectually can't bring themselves to grasp the concept of faith. And that's fine with me. Instead of talking about religion or faith where the Higher Power is concerned, we can talk about spirituality. I contend that whoever and wherever you are as you read these words, you may not have "religion" but you undoubtedly possess spirituality. They are not the same thing, after all.

For the meaning of the word *spiritual*, I returned to the *Oxford English Dictionary* and found: *Of or concerning the spirit as opposed to matter*. That's very clinical, but accurate.

We are all composed of matter, and the proportion of different compounds used to create us has been measured with considerable accuracy. The water, protein, fat, calcium, and other ingredients in our bodies are calculated by volume and mass. The compounds have been broken down to elements, just to make it even more cold and clinical. We're about 65 percent oxygen by mass, 18 percent carbon, and 10 percent hydrogen, with the rest of our weight scattered among trace elements such as potassium, sulphur, and iron. It is within the ability of any chemist to unscramble our body's matter into precise proportions of every element with impressive accuracy. Your body may include 0.35 percent potassium while mine is 0.37 percent potassium and your spouse or partner's may be just 0.33 percent potassium, yet we are all healthy and normal. Hey, we really are different after all!

But think about that for a moment. If your physical being was described according to the portion of various elements that make it up—say, 64.6 percent oxygen, 18.3 percent carbon, 9.8 percent hydrogen, and so on through all the rest of the 60 or so compounds and elements present within us, could you scan the list and say, "Yes, that's me!"?

Of course you couldn't. The physical matter of your body is the "real" you no more than notes on sheets of paper are a Beethoven symphony. It's not the *matter* that defines you and the music. It's the *life* that defines your existence as a human being. In music, the life is the performance. In you, the life is the spirituality. Without the spirituality you are little more than a relatively unique assortment of ingredients. You cannot deny the existence of this life force, this *spirituality*, without running into conflict with, among others, the editors of the *Oxford English Dictionary*. Don't believe me? Read that definition again.

As long as you are enveloped in the emotional impact of your crisis, you are not functioning at the highest potential of your intellectual ability. You are almost certainly functioning well below it, and substantially below that of everyone around you. You have become the dumbest person in the room, and I ask you again:

*Why would you seek wisdom from the dumbest person in the room?*

The Higher Power I employed to bring me through the crisis of alcoholism and the realization that it would soon kill me was my awareness of the people who had gone before me and had succeeded in defeating *their* alcoholism. I knew that if I could follow their lead and tap into their strength—if I did what *they* did—I would be successful. Their achievement was my Higher Power. It was not in the sky, it was not in a holy book, it was not within the walls of a church, temple, mosque, or synagogue. It was in the awareness that others had achieved what I needed to achieve if I were to survive. They were staying sober. They had the power. I would put my faith in what they had accomplished.

Over the years, this concept of the Higher Power that I could trust to guide me through my efforts to fight alcoholism morphed into a sense of a spirit that exists within a room full of achievers. Their achievements could be business oriented or reflective of a personal goal. It didn't matter. When I was in the presence of people who had climbed mythical mountains to reach the peak and change their lives, I could sense the spirit.

Others may offer advice, and you should feel free to absorb it, weigh it, and apply it. But most of us, locked in the emotional impact of our crisis, are ill-equipped to make even those decisions. Think back to Tammy and Larry.

Tammy cannot deal with the wave of crises sweeping over her because she is inundated by their near-simultaneous arrival. She believes that the only way to find peace in her life is to solve all the crises first.

Larry faced one crisis: the breakup of his marriage and the impact it was about to have on almost every aspect of his life. Believing so deeply that this crisis would leave him with nothing to love, he gave serious thought to committing suicide. Yet he dealt with the crisis, made the necessary decisions to move forward with his life, and avoided any further thoughts of suicide.

The key difference between Tammy and Larry and their means of dealing with their personal crises can be summed up this way:

*Tammy believes she can find peace only by first finding a way out of her crises.*

*Larry found a way out of his crisis first by finding peace.*

This is the essence of this book, and the means for dealing with any and all crises you will face in your life: *First find peace.*

FIVE

# Stop Looking Through the Keyhole

*'Tis distance lends enchantment to the view ...*
—THOMAS CAMPBELL, *PLEASURES OF HOPE*, 1799

After three stories of other people's crises, here's one of my own. It may not be as dramatic as Larry's suicidal thoughts, Jennifer's pregnancy, and Tammy's tsunami of challenges, but it was educational and revealing to me; it occurred just as I was writing this book; and it is illustrative of points I expressed earlier.

My wife, Nancy, and I had been out of town for the weekend. I had some business to attend to in another city. It was a two-hour drive away, and we both needed a break from the demands of our home life and the pressure of being parents to two very active teenage girls. With our eldest daughter in residence at university we decided, after much thought and some discussion with our sixteen-year-old, that the younger girl would stay home for the two days we would be absent. Our condominium provides twenty-four-hour security and we had faith in our daughter's assurances that there was nothing to worry about.

The business meeting went well, and Nancy and I enjoyed the all-too-short break. On Sunday morning we were about to begin our drive home when the telephone rang and our housekeeper brought us the kind of news that parents of teenagers dread. Our daughter, we learned, had thrown a party on Saturday night for several friends, and the celebration had spilled over to that morning when the housekeeper arrived. Our home had escaped being trashed to the extent of some news reports we had been hearing recently, but the fact remained that our sixteen-year-old daughter had broken our rule about no parties being held in our absence without our knowledge and approval.

We weren't sure what we could expect to find on our arrival home, but as we began the drive home Nancy and I tossed our angry responses back and forth like a Ping-Pong ball. Most of them were variations on "How could she do this to us??!!" We were, we concluded, victims of a disobedient daughter's actions.

Nancy and I could have built on this mantra over the entire course of the journey, arriving home wrapped in outrage and grim determination to set this wrong right. But we didn't. We were facing, after all, a two-hour drive before reaching home, providing enough time for both of us to calm down, put things in perspective, and reassess our reaction.

At one point I began wondering how my brother Sean would handle things. Sean volunteers much of his time to dealing with adolescents, especially disruptive youths and the challenge they present to their parents. He has served on the executive of parent-support organizations. We have never considered our daughter disruptive, and she has never engaged in some of the more serious activities that these organizations address. But Sean's comments about parenting teenagers, especially when crises develop, resonated with me, and I shared them with Nancy as we drove home.

Here's what Sean had advised: "Never assume the consequences of your children's actions or believe that you are responsible for them" (the actions, not the children, he hastened to add). His next piece of advice appeared especially appropriate: "If you impose new rules, restrictions, and tighter guidelines, you will find yourself sharing the same prison cell with your kids."

In Sean's view, Nancy and I should avoid viewing ourselves as victims of our daughter's actions. "As soon as you see yourself as a victim," Sean had noted, "all your responses are immediately and totally negative. Victims, by nature, are injured, oppressed, destroyed, sacrificed, exploited, tricked, or duped. Victims demand revenge and reparations. They feel insulted and humiliated. There is nothing positive to be gained by considering yourself victimized by the actions of your children."

The long ride home gave Nancy and me an opportunity to discuss and ponder Sean's wisdom and advice. More than that, it helped us dissolve the anger and outrage that had first erupted when we heard of our daughter's unauthorized party. Instead of spending the time in the car growing more and more angry, both of us realized that our role in dealing with this event was to act as the adults, not as the child. When children are victimized by other children, they tend to seek revenge, express anger, and protest about being tricked. They add to the worst aspects of the situation by threatening to balance things with "You did this to me—now watch what *I'm* going to do to *you!*" We didn't need to do this. We needed to be the adults.

We arrived calm and collected, and were met by a contrite daughter who expected a fury of outrage from her parents and who was surprised at our calmness. Nothing had been lost, after all, except a bit of trust, which would be restored with time. More important, Nancy and I felt drawn more closely to her because our daughter was impressed by our composed response to her transgression. We were disappointed, but not outraged. She was remorseful, but not defiant.

Later, I realized that Nancy and I had achieved two things during those few hours in the car returning home.

The first was to find peace through reflecting on the wisdom we had gathered from my brother Sean's experience with family crisis groups. The biggest error that many parents make when responding to a teenage child's transgressions is to overreact, to convince themselves that their child not only cannot be trusted but is destined to a life of failure, misfortune, and possible corruption. Well, it's not really likely. That's just a parent's temporary view through a keyhole.

Nancy and I made what I consider wise decisions on our journey home because, once past our initial outburst, we remained free of the bonds of emotional reaction. We were not the dumbest people in the room. Or, in this case, in the car. Had we succumbed to continued mounting outrage over our daughter's actions, we would have created a wider distance from her, not a closer rapport with her.

The second achievement was to stop looking at things through the keyhole.

When faced with a problem or a challenge, people tend to believe it is important to focus their eyes on it exclusively. This works well when writing an exam, choosing a major appliance, or painting a wall. It doesn't work nearly as well when dealing with the various challenges of life.

Looking through a keyhole limits your view—literally. When you're faced with a serious personal crisis you don't need to limit the things you see. It's the other way around. You need to *widen* your view to take in the whole picture. Instead of looking at the world through a keyhole, you need to take your eye away from the keyhole, swing open the door, and look at the entire room.

In the first few minutes after hearing about our daughter's unauthorized and potentially disastrous party, Nancy and I looked at everything through a keyhole. We could see our anger and disappointment, and little else. Only when we began recalling Sean's observations and reassessing our own knee-jerk response to the news were we able to relax and take a wider view, and this wider view brought us peace. As long as we were, figuratively speaking, bent in front of the door to our lives with one eye pressed against the keyhole, it was impossible for us to absorb and understand everything that was happening. With this awareness came peace. And with peace came a new awareness.

Any time you are dealing with an issue that is important to your happiness and your identity, you will likely tend to narrow your view. This is understandable, but it is also self-defeating.

Concentration is a wonderful skill when playing tennis or writing an exam. But neither of these activities is life. They are only *parts* of life. Life involves options, decisions, risk, opportunity, dedication, disappointment, and a host of other things, and the more deeply you find yourself at a turning point in your life—in a crisis mode, according to the dictionary—the more you gain by taking your eye off the keyhole and looking around at the wider picture.

Sometimes it doesn't take a crisis situation to achieve this. Sometimes it takes only a nudge. Like the one I gave a young man I was sponsoring in a support group several years ago.

The young man's name was Clint and he was a Métis from a small town in Northern Ontario. Only eighteen years old, Clint was fitting all the negative clichés that people often hold about Métis and First Nations people generally, especially those they encounter in our big cities. Raised in a home with a dirt floor, among alcoholic family members in an environment of prejudice and despair, he had everything going against him except his intelligence and determination. Most people wrote Clint off, just as they did others like him. He was, in their parlance, "just another drunken Indian." Actually, he was the antithesis of that racist cliché. Clint was among the most intelligent young people I have ever met, determined to defeat alcohol, and to do something for the Métis and First Nations communities.

On his own, Clint won a scholarship to study social work at a community college just outside Toronto. I met him through the alcoholism support group and sponsored him, providing the support that all alcoholics need to keep their lives in order. One day, while we were walking along the lakeshore near his college, our conversation drifted toward dreams and ambitions. "Forgetting what you are doing right now," I asked Clint, "what would you really dream about doing if you had the opportunity?"

He had already come far, propelled by his intelligence and vision. He could have completed his studies in social work and carried on with a rewarding and credible career as a social worker. That had been his view through the keyhole, and he had no reason to change it until I asked him that question. Perhaps no one else had suggested he express his ambition. Perhaps no one else had given him a reason to stop looking through the keyhole in exchange for a wider vision.

Whatever the reason, I will never forget Clint stopping, thinking over my words, and finally saying, "I have always wanted to be a lawyer able to help my people back home," meaning his birthplace far to the north. Then he shrugged and added, "But I don't have the education, I don't have the skills, I don't have a lot of things I need to get into law school."

I don't believe he had expressed this ambition aloud before. But having said it made the dream not only realistic but possible. He saw the possibility when he pulled himself away from the keyhole; he looked around and discovered a pre-law program for First Nations people in Saskatchewan. Within thirty days he was enrolled in the course. He completed it with excellent marks and as a result was accepted as a law student at York University's Osgoode Hall Law School. Graduating in the top quarter of his class, he was immediately hired by one of the country's largest and most prestigious law firms.

We stayed in touch through the early years of Clint's law career. When the legal firm opened a Vancouver office to deal primarily with First Nations claims he was chosen to help launch it, and when one of the country's largest chartered banks needed a legal counsel to handle complex deals with investment derivatives, they offered the position to Clint.

He and I met for lunch one day when he was back in Toronto in the employ of the bank. "My job is totally secure," he said with a smile after describing his work to me. When I asked what made him so certain about his job security he said, "Because I'm the only person in the place who really understands what these derivatives are all about!" As I said, he is a very bright guy.

He is also a determined guy who marches to the beat of his own drum. With his law degree, his experience with a major legal firm, and his banking connections, Clint could have continued his climb out of a dirt-floor hut into a solid position among the country's elite business establishment. But that had never been his dream. His dream, he reminded himself and me after mentioning how secure his job was, was to serve the Métis and First Nations communities. And that's precisely what he did.

Soon after our lunch, Clint walked away from his luxurious downtown office and moved back to northwestern Ontario, where he opened a law office in a small building in his hometown about 120 miles north of Lake Superior. He and his legal staff provide services to First Nations and their agencies and businesses in the region, covering governance, business ventures, treaty rights and land claims, child welfare, and general points of law as they apply to First Nations peoples. And Clint was right: He still knows so much about financial derivatives that he continues to work for the bank in that capacity, online from his office.

I love this story because it is real, because I played a small role in Clint's achievements, and because it's about a dream come true for a worthy guy. It also represents an indisputable truth: When you remove your eye from the keyhole that limits both your view and your options, you discover worlds of choice that you did not know existed. Because you couldn't see them.

Clint was not deeply embedded in an emotional crisis when I spoke to him while walking along the lakeshore. He was not entirely at peace with himself, either. He had achieved a great deal by overcoming prejudice, poverty, peer influences, and a host of other challenges that most urban-dwelling non-Native people can hardly fathom. But he wanted to become more than a social worker, as important as that work might be. He also *knew* he was capable of becoming more and doing more. No one, I gather, had proposed that he expand his horizons and search for ways to achieve his ambition to practice law for aboriginal people until I made the suggestion while we were strolling along the lakeshore that day.

Once Clint discovered that his ambitious goal might be within reach after all, I believe he reacted with two contrasting emotions. One was to find peace in the absence of the frustration he had been feeling for many years, based on his perceived limited opportunity. The other was to fuel a fierce determination to see that the opportunity was not wasted, and that his idealistic dream of serving his people could indeed be realized. And it was.

Each of us encounters challenges and obstacles in our lives, some momentary and others ongoing. Yet our natural inclination is to be relatively at peace with ourselves and with those around us. That's the posture of, for want of a better term, *normal people*. It is normal to desire peace in our lives. Anyone who is constantly tearing at the fabric of his or her being, prepared to battle the world and everyone in it, is not grappling with a crisis but with a serious mental illness.

It is in your nature to move through life in a manner that makes you comfortable with yourself and with those around you whose company you value and enjoy. To draw upon an earlier phrase, peace is the default position of people's lives, the one you seek even in the midst of conflict. The biggest problem many of us face in dealing with personal crises is finding peace, yet peace is always available. Your reaction to the crisis you face is the only barrier to finding the peace you need to deal with the crisis. If you control your emotional reaction, you will find the peace you need.

With peace, the keyhole expands. You see a wider view, you understand more of the situation, and you grasp the knowledge of what to do.

Our experience with our daughter having a party while we were away wasn't much of a crisis compared with those confronting Larry, Jennifer, and Tammy. Nevertheless, it qualified as a turning point, the definition of a crisis. As my brother Sean puts it, raising teenagers is often a series of crises big and small, and too many parents are ill-equipped to handle them. Not the teenagers—the crises.

Many people have difficulty handling personal crises of *any* magnitude, and Sean provided me with a few examples drawn from his work on behalf of parents' assistance groups.

When parents of a troubling teenager sought assistance from parent-support groups, Sean and the other counselors tended to ignore the specific complaint. In their view, the complaint said more about the parents' view than about their child's actions.

A typical concern might be: "He always comes in late, after his curfew, especially on weekends. He shows up at two or three in the morning, and goes into the kitchen to make himself something to eat. And it keeps happening over and over."

Instead of suggesting ways to control the teenager's late hours, the counselors would begin by asking the parents to visualize their child's situation five years in the future. Where did they want to see their son or daughter at that point?

The answers were predictable. "I would hope she's enrolled in a good college or university, getting good grades, and working toward whatever career she wants to follow" was typical. Another was a variation of "I would like him to be in a good relationship with a young woman, the two of them planning their future together" or "It wouldn't matter to me as long as he is happy with his life and with himself."

Sean and the other counselors would respond by saying, "But none of your hopes for your son or daughter included being punctual. Why should this be bothering you now? What's really at the heart of your concern?"

This was a means of pulling the parents' eyes away from the keyhole to deal with a wider view. In the case of the teenage boy making himself something to eat in the middle of the night, the parents might complain that the noise of him rattling around in the kitchen woke them up, and they resented the intrusion on their sleep.

"So if you weren't awakened by these late-night snack preparations," the counselors would ask, "would things be better for you?"

Assuming this was the parents' principal complaint about their child's behavior, the reply would usually be an agreement that, yes, as long as they weren't awakened by the noise, they would accept the situation. The teenager arriving late wasn't the real problem. The real problem was the parents' frequent loss of a good night's sleep. Various solutions presented themselves: keeping the kitchen and bedroom doors closed, or even considering earplugs.

One of the most common complaints involved teenagers' housekeeping habits. "He never cleans his room!" the parents would say with enormous frustration. "It's a terrible mess. We're tired of cleaning it up and we're even more tired of looking at it day after day."

The counselors would remind parents that almost no one, by the time they are in their mid-twenties, maintains their living quarters in the same state they did when they were in their mid-teens. It's one more measure of maturity, and parents should accept that things almost certainly will improve with time. Their children know the right thing to do, parents would be reminded. They are simply not in a state of mind, as adolescents, to do it. Not yet. They will enter that state of mind in adulthood.

"But we have to look at it every time we pass his room!" the parents might answer, to which Sean and the other counselors would reply, "No, you don't have to look at it. You can solve the problem by just closing the door."

This isn't a matter of a parent abdicating responsibility where their adolescent child is concerned. It's a matter of finding peace instead of being buried in frustration and anger, and knowing that peace brings with it the opportunity and wisdom to solve the problem. It is, if you prefer, a means of letting go.

In some cases the problem appeared more serious, such as receiving a late-night telephone call from the police department announcing that the parents' teenage child was in custody for a relatively minor charge such as trespassing. This kind of message tends to send parents into an emotional orbit. Things grow more fiery when Mom and Dad jump into the car and drive at the speed limit, exchanging threats of what they are going to do when they get their hands on their child. A call from the police! In the middle of the night! How humiliating! Their arrival at the police station usually starts with apologies to the police officers followed by angry words and threats to the child. Back home there may be shouts, warnings, slamming doors, and cold silence.

When things begin to settle down, other problems arise. Both parents may begin to feel guilty about their actions and assume they have failed as parents. Fathers tend to consider this a blow to their ego ("How could he/she do this to me?!") while mothers wish to forgive the child and search for reasons to blame themselves ("What am I doing wrong?!"). This dichotomy creates a new level of conflict; now, in addition to the parents expressing outrage over the actions of their teen, they begin disagreeing with each other about the best methods of approaching the problem.

In search of a solution, and a better means of handling the situation should it arise again, many parents seek help from the counseling group. At the meetings their frustration builds in the telling of the story—the call from the police station ("What will the neighbors think if they find out?"), the drive to the police station ("We grew angrier and angrier!"), the attitude of their child when they arrived ("He/she just didn't take the whole thing seriously!"), and finally a summation of the situation ("We can't control our kid!").

The last statement can be the most revealing, and provides the opening for the most valuable lesson to be learned. Upon hearing the core of the complaint—*We can't control our kid!*—the parents need to be reminded gently of a fact of life they have been ignoring: You can't control *anybody*.

Control should not be the issue where children are concerned. In fact, it should not be the issue in any relationship. No one should attempt to control someone else in a mutually beneficial relationship. You should not accept the idea of control among adults, and it is foolish to accept or promote it among parents and children. The only important thing to accomplish during these counseling sessions is to create peace within the family. When peace is established or restored—when each family member has moved beyond his or her emotional response to whatever was considered a threat—the solutions become apparent.

"So what should we do if it happens again?" the parents might demand. "How can we handle the situation better if, heaven forbid, we're faced with the same situation?" It all comes down to removing the parents' eyes from the keyhole.

First, the counselors advise, take a neutral stance. There is no need to defend either your child's actions, the actions of the police, or your own response.

Second, realize that your child's actions did not directly involve you. The child does not have or should not have a problem with you as the parents. His or her problem is with society, and that's how it should be addressed.

Finally, the most important suggestion: Let your child deal with the situation alone, to the fullest possible extent. When the police inform parents that their child is being held for some minor misdemeanor and will be released to the parents' custody, the parents' response should not be to rush to the station and collar their son or daughter, building their anger and frustration along the way. They should say to the police officer or whoever informs them of the situation, "Thank you very much. Please take good care of him/her, and we will be there to pick her/him up at eight in the morning."

This may generate surprise and even disagreement on the part of the police. So what? It provides the parents with a chance to sidestep the buildup of anger that is almost certain to occur if their response is immediate and brash. It also provides the child with a chance to reflect on the situation, and dramatically changes the scenario when the parents confront their child in the morning.

There is no reason to berate the child when the parents arrive at the police station. The teenager has already been berated simply by being arrested. The best way is to greet the child by expressing sorrow or disappointment about his or her problems with the police—not *the parents'* problems—offer a hug, and maybe breakfast. If the child has to make a later appearance in court or with a police officer as a result of the situation, he or she should be reminded about it once, and not again. "You have not been hired to be your child's calendar or secretary," the counselors tell parents. "Don't remind him/her of his/her responsibilities. Notify the child just once. Then it becomes the child's concern."

This attitude has been described in the past, by other sources, as *tough love*. Perhaps it is, but the term suggests that the actions are child-centered, and that's not entirely correct. While we all love and wish to protect our children, we cannot do this if we are locked into the restrictive view of a keyhole and if we are not at peace within our own mind.

Dealing with crises created by teenagers resonates especially well with me because I generated a period of near-constant crises for my parents. By the time I entered my mid-teen years, I was already an alcoholic. You may not consider alcoholism to be an ailment of young people. The clichéd image of an alcoholic is a man stumbling down a sidewalk searching for money to purchase a bottle of cheap wine, or a woman concealing a bottle in her desk drawer, constantly sipping from it to get through the day. A middle-class kid from a stable home environment doesn't sound like the usual suspect for an alcoholic personality.

But that was me. A boy who did well in school (for a while ...), with parents and siblings who were vibrant and supportive (again, for a while ...), yet who stole money from his mother's purse, wrecked his father's automobiles, and generally terrorized his brothers and sister with his self-destructive behavior. Whenever my actions attracted the attention of the police and my parents received the dreaded late-night call, they dutifully found their way to the police station, brought me home, and reminded me of my obligation to make amends of some sort.

Their keyhole view of me showed them a bad kid, a boy who didn't give a damn about his family, his friends, or himself. To my parents, I had been born rebellious and would stay that way until, they hoped, I matured and began acting responsibly. Like my brothers and sister. Why couldn't I be like them and like the teenage sons of their friends?

If they had been able to widen their view of me, they would have known the reason. They would have discovered that I had been sexually assaulted at age thirteen by an older woman, and that this assault was followed by a brutal rape by a Montreal police officer and, on different occasions, by two Catholic priests.

These incidents, traumatic as they were, are not an excuse for my behavior and the pain I caused my parents and siblings. I take responsibility for those actions. But had my parents been able to view the Frank O'Dea behind the crazy kid whose only ambition was to become as drunk as possible each day of his life, they would have found an answer to my actions and understood how they may have helped me.

Through almost all my teenage years, I was my parents' personal crisis. They kept their eyes to the keyhole, seeing me as a thoroughly rebellious teenager acting without regard for their happiness (which was true) or for my own welfare (also true), and for no rational reason (not entirely true). They could not understand what was really happening to me until they found peace. Unfortunately they grew convinced that they could only find peace by waiting for me to solve my problem myself or, when this appeared to prove unlikely, by banishing me from the family.

Finding peace expands the keyhole through which you are watching the world and watching yourself deal with your crisis. You cannot grasp all the means available to handle the crisis by keeping your eye on the keyhole. And you cannot remove your eye from the keyhole until you find peace.

# SIX

# The Next Right Thing

*You come into the world alone and you go out of
the world alone yet it seems to me you are
more alone while living than even going and coming.*
—EMILY CARR

Whenever a crisis occurs to someone close to you, you may tend to project the same challenge onto yourself, perhaps seeing it as a harbinger of problems that could strike you. It's a standard illustration of the fear of an unknown future, usually without basis in fact, and it's a challenge to you when you're seeking the peace you need to deal with your situation. In preparing my thoughts for this book, I found no shortage of examples to use. Krystal's was a classic.

After months of denying what her instincts had been telling her, Krystal finally accepted the truth that her son Mitchell was addicted to drugs, and either was unwilling or unable to stop using them. This was bad enough, but she had recently discovered evidence that he was also dealing drugs as a means of supporting his habit.

A single mother, Krystal already faced her own challenges. She had been worrying about her financial situation, her job security, and her health. The previous year, a mammogram had revealed a small growth in one breast, leading to a lumpectomy and radiation therapy. Her physician assured her that the prospects for remaining cancer-free looked good, but the experience had been understandably upsetting.

"One good thing that I thought might come from my surgery and treatment," she said, "was that it would make Mitchell grow up. I could tell that he was really shaken up about me being treated for cancer. I saw him cry, and he told his aunt, my sister, that he didn't know what he would do if I died. So I figured, when I got a clean bill of health from my doctor, that he would come out of this changed. For the better." Then she shrugged. "Obviously, I was wrong."

Krystal had reason to be optimistic about her son in the long term. Mitchell was an intelligent boy who had no problem achieving good marks in his schoolwork. He even talked to her about his plans to become a teacher, an idea that had thrilled Krystal. This stuff with drugs was just a phase, she believed. He would soon grow out of it.

She realized he hadn't when Mitchell arrived home late one night with a bloodied nose and bruises on his body. When Krystal asked what had happened to him and prepared to drive him to a hospital for medical treatment, he refused her help. He had been injured, he explained, trying to ride a friend's skateboard down some concrete steps. He lost control and fell against a fence. After a shower he would be fine, and he promised he wouldn't try that again.

But Krystal was a nurse. She knew the difference between injuries caused by a fall from a skateboard and wounds that were the result of a beating. "Who beat you up?" she asked.

Mitchell was so surprised by the directness and accuracy of her question that he muttered, "Some guy …"

"Why?" Krystal demanded. When Mitchell refused to respond she asked, "A drug deal?" Mitchell's quick retreat into his room appeared to give her the answer.

Later that week when Krystal told her story to a parents' group she emphasized her love for her son, and praised his intelligence and abilities. She was actually harder on herself than on her son. She questioned the hands-off attitude she had taken toward her son over the past year. "I thought at first it was just a teenage thing, smoking dope and hanging out with people I didn't like," she said tearfully. "Then I became wrapped up with my cancer treatment and couldn't give him all the attention he needed." The confirmation that he was selling drugs to other students and the deep suspicion that he had been beaten over a drug deal gone wrong created panic within her. Mitchell, she tried to explain, was neither lacking in intelligence nor a criminal. He missed his father, who lived on the other side of the country and rarely contacted Mitchell, and he had been on his own too much while Krystal received medical treatment.

The idea that her son could face serious criminal charges was terrifying to her. But so was the chance that he could be seriously injured by other dealers. There was more: She had heard stories of dealers invading homes in search of drugs and money they feel is owed them. Was that what might happen? Would she and Mitchell confront thugs waving guns and knives in their apartment some evening? And what about her friends and neighbors? She would feel crushed and humiliated if Mitchell were to be arrested for selling drugs.

One of the most difficult challenges you may face in the midst of a crisis is making a firm decision to change your views and your actions, even when you know it is in your best interest. Sometimes you may resist change because you are unsure of the result. You may even take comfort in accepting a bad situation, a bad relationship, even a bad life because, you fear, change might cause it to become even worse. You suffer from the same emotional handicap that paralyzed and depressed Larry back in chapter 1: You fear the future even though you recognize that change has already taken place—the past is gone, the present is unfolding, and a different future awaits whether you are ready or not.

Eventually you ignore the unease that change brings and, in the words of the popular advertising slogan, "Just do it." By that time other problems may have developed, and the changes you need to make may have become more difficult.

Once you accept that you are in the midst of a crisis, and that things are about to change despite your desire that they remain as they were, you need to adapt to the new reality. By taking the initiative at the right time, you can exert some influence on your life before being persuaded that you have no other choice.

Mitchell's situation is not like the ones that Sean described earlier, when he spoke of parents who encounter typical teenager issues such as skipping classes or shoplifting. If Mitchell is operating with major drug wholesalers, she fears he may be risking his life. Has Krystal's hands-off approach to her son's activities helped put him in serious danger? It is clear to me that Krystal is almost certainly feeling guilty about her concern with her own health crisis. If she had not been paying so much attention to the treatment she needed to deal with her breast cancer, she may be thinking, perhaps she could have diverted Mitchell from his involvement in drugs and eliminated the crisis entirely.

With all due respect to Krystal's intelligence and opinion, this is nonsense. She provided her son with love, attention, and a model of behavior as a single parent, teaching him by example lessons of responsibility and achievement. She has no need to feel any guilt at all about the choices her son appears to have made. Nor should she feel inhibited and embarrassed about any judgments that friends and neighbors may make about her son. They may, in fact, be dealing with similar behavior by their own children.

Parents will confirm that dealing with the actions of teenagers, especially where drugs and other such illegal activities are concerned, is enormously difficult. As a single working mother, Krystal has to manage other concerns as well.

Underlying everything is the natural impulse to resist change until it is unavoidable. We all harbor this reluctance to deal with change, even when we recognize the need. Sometimes reluctance is the result of addiction. Every heavy smoker and every alcoholic knows the need to change his or her actions; logic and awareness tell them so, yet still they resist. Much of this resistance is rooted in the unique nature of addictive personalities, but it cannot be denied that the source of their inability to change their habits is tied to the same reluctance we all share.

Krystal was not blind to Mitchell's actions in the past. She was aware of his drug use, although not of his relationship with dealers who were prepared to punish him physically. Faced with the crisis of discovering Mitchell's injuries and knowing instinctively how they were caused, her challenge is not to admit what she has known all along to be true, but to overcome her fear of moving from the old—ignoring Mitchell's actions with the hope that it's a passing phase, the probable result of peer pressure—to the new, which means taking a more active role in her son's life.

At the moment, Krystal has no way of identifying what the new role should be. And she won't be able to make any decision in her current state. Choosing what to do, and finding the strength to carry it through, will take more willpower than Krystal has to draw upon on her own.

It is understandable for Krystal to feel she needs to do something—but what?

When Krystal begins to understand that she cannot change anyone's behavior except her own, she will take the first step toward doing the next right thing. Again:

*You cannot control anyone.* You can, however, control your own reactions.

Anything Krystal attempts to do to directly control her son's actions is doomed to failure. Neither threats nor nagging him will help. Both are likely to drive them further apart. The most valuable asset they appear to have at the moment is their apparent closeness, and she should not risk destroying this level of intimacy between the two of them.

Krystal cannot control her son's behavior, but she can and must control the environment in which they live. This includes a total ban on any drugs in their home. There must be an understanding that she will destroy any drugs she finds in their apartment without regard for ownership. This does more than make it difficult for Mitchell to function as a dealer. It provides an island of safety for him, where his environment will not be invaded by the source of his troubles. Will it prevent Mitchell from using drugs himself? Probably not. But it will provide both him and his mother with a refuge from their influence.

The primary barrier to Krystal doing what she knows in her heart she must do is her various fears, including:

*Fear of the unknown.* Krystal knows what to do. She may not know how to do it, but she knows what must be done. She lacks, unfortunately, assurance that her actions will improve her relationship with Mitchell. No one can guarantee they will. But she is about to enter unexplored territory. To this point she has been a supportive, even indulgent mother to her son. Now she must change that role for his own good. How will he react? Will it bring him closer or drive him away? She doesn't know, and she fears not knowing.

We often make up fears to fill gaps in our knowledge. Krystal's fear of her son being seriously injured by drug dealers may be overblown. Police officers dealing with adolescent use of drugs find it rare for this to happen. It's not impossible, simply less likely than Krystal believes.

*Fear of upsetting others.* This is an extension of the first fear, but more specific. Krystal's actions are not likely to be welcomed by Mitchell. She does not want to upset him. She hates the thought of the anger he is likely to express—the shouts, the tantrums, the harsh words. Of course, the possibility also exists that he may welcome her assistance. Again, she doesn't know.

*Fear of leaving a comfort zone.* Obviously, Mitchell's actions have disturbed Krystal. The risk of his facing serious injury and perhaps a jail sentence as a result of dealing drugs disturbs her. Things have been going so well lately. Her work at the clinic has been praised, and she has been encouraged to start new training that could move her into a supervisory position. Her finances are more settled than they have ever been, and her social life is the best it has been since her marriage ended. Tackling Mitchell's problems, she fears, will cause more than headaches for her. It might disturb her life in a manner that would be difficult to accept. She has to do something to help her son, of course, but still …

Remember: At least 90 percent of the future events that we fear never happen.

Krystal's situation is an example of the need to step aside and seek strength from a Higher Power. The best place to look for this power may be within herself. She has, after all, achieved much as a single parent, including surviving cancer. Somewhere within Krystal is a power greater than she recognizes. It needn't be identified or named, only acknowledged and trusted. Through this decision alone, she can and will find peace. With peace she will grasp the next right thing to do.

This concept of doing "the next right thing" confuses some people. "Are you suggesting that as soon as I find peace," they ask, "a door will open, and behind it I will discover a guide to doing what I was supposed to do all along, and never saw before? Is *that* what you're suggesting?"

Yes. As a matter of fact, that is exactly what I am suggesting.

Consider the view through the keyhole of a closed door that you insist on seeing in the midst of a crisis. Behind the closed door may be the best way out of your crisis, but as long as your view is through the small keyhole exclusively and not through a wide open door, how will you see it? You cannot take your eye from the keyhole while you are in crisis mode, the mode linked to the evolutionary fight-or-flight response.

You desperately need to find peace by first placing yourself and your situation in the hands of a Higher Power. Then step back from the keyhole and wait for the door to open. And it will.

I found a good demonstration of this in the story of a woman I'll call Marie-Therese.

Marie-Therese's husband, Pierre, had been a thoughtful and caring man who had a large insurance policy with Marie-Therese as the beneficiary. He had also accumulated a substantial balance in his retirement savings plan. "When we're sixty years old," he had boasted to Marie-Therese, "we're both going to quit working and start to enjoy life. Especially travel. We'll go to all those places we wanted to visit, like South America and Australia. We'll spend winters where it's warm and go walking on the beach every day. In the summer we'll play golf together, and during the seasons in between we'll sit around and plan our next trip!"

THE NEXT RIGHT THING

But there was no next trip—or even a first. When Pierre was driving home one night from his work as manager of a fast-food restaurant, his car was struck by a drunk driver who had raced at high speed through a red light. Pierre died instantly, two months before his fiftieth birthday.

Marie-Therese was lost in her sorrow. She had built her life around her husband and the dreams they had shared. In the middle of her grieving, she was contacted by Jean-Claude, an in-law of Pierre's cousin.

"The best way to honor Pierre's dreams," Jean-Claude told Marie-Therese, holding her hand and speaking in a soft, understanding voice, "is to make the most of the legacy he has left you. Then, when you choose to leave your teaching job, you will have the money to do whatever you want to do, go wherever you want to go, all in first class."

Jean-Claude's investment firm, he promised her, would manage the almost $600,000 in insurance and retirement funds that Pierre had left, building it in value over the years. Her money would be invested carefully in stocks, bonds, and mutual funds, and she would receive statements every six months showing the growth of her account. It would be safe and well-managed, and would increase at a steady rate year by year. By the time Marie-Therese was sixty years old, he assured her, the account could be worth more than $1 million.

Two years from age sixty, Marie-Therese discovered that her account was worth nothing. As he had been doing with his other clients, Jean-Claude took Marie-Therese's money for his own use, financing a gambling addiction and a lifestyle that included three houses, several fancy cars, and trips abroad with friends and relatives. The statements she had been receiving from Jean-Claude, showing a steady increase in the savings and insurance left to her by Pierre, were a total fiction. The police investigators expected none of his clients would recover a penny of their investments.

The money was gone, all $10 million entrusted to Jean-Claude by Marie-Therese and his other clients. She would be retiring in two years, and while she would be entitled to a teacher's pension, it would be relatively small. She would survive, but she would not travel to the places she had dreamed of visiting, even without Pierre. She might not even be able to maintain her home on her pension.

Like all victims of this kind of crime, Marie-Therese suffered on two levels. The first was the loss of the financial future that she and her husband had worked so hard to secure. They had sacrificed in various ways to ensure that they would not be a burden to anyone, and that they could look forward to their years of retirement. It vanished because they had placed their trust in the wrong place or, more correctly, in the wrong person.

She suffered in another way as well. After Pierre's death, she had been grateful for the manner in which he had taken charge of their future. He had done it, she believed, out of love for her and in anticipation of the years they expected to spend together. Now, along with all the other emotions she was feeling, Marie-Therese was lost in guilt and betrayal—not due to the actions of Jean-Claude, but to her own decisions. She felt guilty about believing Jean-Claude's promises, and she felt she had betrayed Pierre by destroying the fruits of his planning and hard work.

When I learned of Marie-Therese's situation, she was still staggered by what had happened to her and the money. Neither eating nor sleeping well, she had withdrawn from friends and family, and taken a long-term leave from her profession. Teaching a class was out of the question. She felt emotionally paralyzed and risked spending the rest of her life pondering what she had lost and punishing herself for her misplaced trust.

I was as saddened by Marie-Therese's misfortune as I'm sure you are. My feelings were not going to help her through her crisis, however. She needed to know the next right thing to do.

One of the most difficult aspects of her crisis was handling her guilt over Jean-Claude's criminal actions. She blamed herself for placing her trust in a man who did not deserve it. She felt that her misplaced trust had stained the memory of the love and concern for her that Pierre had expressed by building the nest egg for the future they would never share.

Dealing with a personal crisis is difficult enough without carrying a heavy burden of guilt. Marie-Therese's personal crisis was more than financial, and its impact was certain to be deep and long lasting. You may agree that she had no reason to blame herself for the illegal and inhumane actions of someone else, but you are not in Marie-Therese's shoes. Blaming herself for the loss may not be logical, but it is understandable.

There was no sunshine to be found in Marie-Therese's story. She had been the victim of an unscrupulous individual who could legitimately be labeled a sociopath for his actions. Unfortunately, there are more people like him around. It's also certain that there are more people like Marie-Therese around, whose trust will be misplaced and who will pay the price for it in many ways.

Many of these people never permit themselves to be happy again, because they believe their sorrow and resentment are a method of punishing the individual who robbed them of their money. It's a foolish idea. Neither Jean-Claude nor anyone who would commit such a crime would care about their victims' sorrow and losses. These criminals are highly narcissistic. They could not care less about their victims or their victims' opinions of them because they have either a repressed conscience or no conscience at all. Without an active conscience, criminals cannot feel guilt, and without guilt, there is no remorse.

Marie-Therese was wise enough to resist focusing on Jean-Claude's greed and criminal behavior. She needed peace, and through small steps she found it by counting the good things in her life, the parts of her life that no one could take from her. These included her health, which remained good; her friends, who rallied around her; her teaching, and the students who responded to her attention and advice, assuring her of their respect for her; her faith, which had been shaken but not shattered by Jean-Claude's betrayal; and memories of her husband, Pierre. "I sometimes feel he talks to me at night while I am sleeping," she said, "telling me not to blame myself for what happened. So I leave it to Pierre to settle things, not me. My family thinks I'm crazy when I say it's all in Pierre's and God's hands, but that's what I do. Together they represent a Higher Power to me."

She smiled when she remembered some things she and Pierre used to say to each other. "Before we were married, when I told him I wasn't sure if I wanted to get married right away because I wanted to travel before becoming a teacher, Pierre would say *'C'est plus important que chacun de nous.'* [This is bigger than both of us.] He meant the way we felt about each other. I used to laugh at him, telling him he sounded like somebody from a *téléroman* [a soap opera]. Well, maybe he was right. He loved me enough to make plans for both of us together, and when I started to tell myself that his love for me was not only bigger than the money Jean-Claude took from me and others, but that it was also something that neither Jean-Claude nor anybody else could ever take from me, well, that's when I said I would trust his love."

She smiled again and said, "I'm not sure Father, at my church, agrees completely, but he said that whatever I depended on to help me forgive and find peace was okay with him."

Day by day Marie-Therese moved away from her fears and from her despair over the loss of her retirement nest egg. When she was once again at peace, she resumed her teaching and her life. She loved teaching almost as much, she explained, as she loved Pierre, and concentrating on the profession she loved was the next right thing to do. So she did it.

I have no doubt that a Higher Power exists for everyone. However you define it, and wherever you locate it, accepting a Higher Power represents the essential first step toward leaving your current crisis behind. For those of you who are closely in touch with your spirituality, relying on a Higher Power for strength is easy and almost instantaneous. For others, it may be more difficult.

Here's what I think:

*Time spent questioning the existence of a Higher Power and searching for reasons to reject the concept is time wasted.* Meaning, you will remain mired in the pain and uncertainty of your crisis longer than necessary. Instead of refusing to search for a Higher Power that will help you through your crisis, try traveling to some place where *it* can find *you*.

Here are seven ways you might encounter your Higher Power. Don't expect it/he/she to leap out from behind a rock to surprise you, or to slide down a sunbeam toward you. Things don't happen that way. You will know you have encountered your Higher Power when you find peace, and when you find peace you will be prepared to do the next right thing:

1.  *Accept what is.* We cannot change the world or our past. We are rarely good even at changing ourselves. Larry could not change the end of his marriage, Jennifer could not wish away her pregnancy, and Marie-Therese could not bring back the money that Jean-Claude had embezzled. You must accept those things you cannot change and focus on the things that you are able to influence. This does two things: It eliminates the time-wasting, soul-destroying futility of focusing on an impossible task; and it provides you with a sense of power when you begin addressing the aspects of your life that you can control to some degree.

2.  *Spend time in nature.* Cities are wonderful, stimulating places but they are rarely serene. Serenity brings peace, and vice versa. If you have easy access to the countryside—a dense woods in summer is ideal—walk among the trees, and immerse yourself

in silence as often as you are able. If you need to drive to the countryside, do so, but don't attempt to sample the experience from inside your car. Park your car, find a nature trail, and, if you are physically able, set out to absorb all that nature offers. If you are stuck in the city, look for a large park to explore. Choose a place where you feel safe when alone. The security of a friend's company may be necessary, but the kind of peaceful environment I'm proposing is best absorbed in solitude.

3. *Care about others.* In the midst of a crisis that consumes us emotionally, it is difficult to appreciate the challenges and problems faced by others. They exist, however, and one of the best ways to locate inner peace is to immerse yourself for a time in other people's problems with the aim of aiding them. You can offer assistance to family and friends who appear to need it, or to strangers through a volunteer group. One of the immediate benefits of helping others is that it places your current crisis in perspective. It's quite possible that your problems may not appear so overwhelming after you have assisted others in dealing with theirs.

4. *Learn about the world.* You don't have all the answers to life, and you never will. But the more you learn about the things you do, and why you do them, the better you will feel about your own situation. Many people find solace in learning about science, or studying obscure subjects such as Renaissance

music or abstract art. The subject you choose doesn't matter, only that it holds interest for you. What matters is your ability to open your mind to other things besides your current concerns, and pull your eye away from the keyhole.

5. *Live in the present moment.* In the midst of a crisis that overwhelms you, you often regret the past and fear the future. Once again: The past is something you cannot change (see #1, above), and the future is something you should not fear because whatever frightens you may not come to pass. If you live in the present moment, free of regrets and fear, you discover stillness. Stillness brings peace.

6. *Consider meditation.* Be skeptical if you wish, but millions of people find that meditation enables them to clear their minds of debris and focus their attention on things that truly matter. (Remember that hamster wheel that keeps spinning in a mind that cannot find peace? Meditation stops the wheel and frees the hamster.) In that sense, it is an excellent means of letting the Higher Power find you, or the other way around. Try this and see if it works for you: Take twenty minutes to sit back in a comfortable chair in a silent, dimly lit room. Close your eyes and try to empty your mind. Let your thoughts come and go across your consciousness. Focus on the emptiness that remains. When you open your eyes and turn your attention to the things that occupied you earlier, they will appear different

to you—clearer, sharper, more colorful, less frightening, and more accessible.

7. *Cherish hope.* Try never to lose the things you cherish
   most in life. Hope can show you the path toward
   peace. Even if your hope is based only on the awareness that the sun is always shining behind the clouds,
   it will be enough for you to hold on to. Without
   hope, you are doomed. With hope, you will survive.

Finding peace enables you to pull yourself away from the view
through the keyhole and look around. When you do, you discover
options you had not been able to see before. Among them is
the next right thing to do. At that point you are able to make a
decision, and making a good decision is the essential first step to
dealing with a crisis.

Finding the next right thing to do leads to making a "good"
decision. Don't count on making a perfect or even a "pure"
decision, meaning a decision you make without any outside
influences or secondary concerns. There are no perfect or pure
decisions, only right decisions. When your eye is no longer glued
to that keyhole you will always know what that right decision is,
and then what to do.

Here is something else you can count on:

*The right thing to do is almost always the hardest thing to do.*

Surprised? You shouldn't be. If it were the easiest thing to do,
you would have accomplished it long ago. You may not want to
know the next right thing to do, and you may not want to hear
why you should do it. Knowing what it is and why you should do

it may not be enough incentive for you to get it done. Not right away. But it is the only way to deal with a crisis and ensure that the outcome is in your favor.

Standing in the chill of a December morning all those years ago, waiting to beg money for the bottle of wine I needed to get through the day, was easy for me. It was almost Christmas, after all. Surely people would be generous on a day so close to Christmas. I had stood on a street corner like this hundreds of times, begging for spare change to pay for a bottle of wine. The wine would save me for another day.

Giving up the only way of life that appeared to bring me solace would not be easy. But in the brief moment when I found peace—when peace arrived with the realization that I needed something or somebody bigger than myself—I knew what the next right thing to do would be. In the state of mind that had enveloped me for many years up to that point, I could not have recognized the next right thing. In a sudden moment of peace, it became clear to me. And it may have been the most difficult thing I've ever done in my life.

I consider myself a spiritual person, but I am not one who can easily accept strange occurrences popping up at precisely the right time. Only in fairy tales do genies rise out of old lamps to grant three wishes. Yet each time I have emerged from the core of a crisis into a state of peace, having decided to do the next right thing, a solution has appeared. Do I have an angel sitting on my shoulder, guiding me in just the right direction at just the right time? I doubt it.

Instead, my explanation is to accept that the solution to problems connected with my crisis has always been there. I couldn't see it until I found peace, took my eye away from the keyhole, and did the next right thing. That's the process and that's how it works. It works for me, it can work for the people whose crises we have examined in this book, and it can work for you as well.

You can't be in their shoes entirely, but consider the people you have met so far—Larry, whose wife's announcement that their marriage was over sent him into a near-suicidal tailspin; Jennifer, whose pregnancy threatened to end her career plans as well as her relationship with her parents; Tammy, who faced a series of crises that might have overwhelmed her entirely; Krystal, who needed to deal with her son's involvement in drugs and drug trafficking; and Marie-Therese, who needed to get past the terrible crime inflicted upon her and enjoy the rest of her life without many of the things she had planned to enjoy.

Without making decisions for them, reflect on how they should handle the situations they've faced. Put them and yourself in a place of peace, where the threats and challenges can no longer reach them and you.

Now ponder the right thing to do—the thing that, in the comfort of your peace of mind, is the obvious choice. This is the way out of the crisis. It is the way out of every crisis.

SEVEN

# We Are Never Fully Trapped

*The blame is his who chooses: God is blameless.*
—PLATO

As I noted earlier, the next right thing is rarely the easiest thing to do among all the options you may have. But once you have found peace and can see the wider view of your situation, you always know what it is. You also know that it is the only practical route out of the crisis in which you find yourself.

What prevents you from doing the next right thing after you identify it? Aside from the fact that it's rarely easy to do, it almost always includes suffering a blow or two to your pride. No big surprise there. The more pride you take in your life's achievements, the more difficult it is to let go of them or accept a change in their status.

In *When All You Have Is Hope*, I explained how Tom Culligan and I built Second Cup (based on an idea we had while sampling ice cream at a Baskin-Robbins counter) into a pioneering enterprise in brewing and marketing gourmet coffee. Through franchising we made Second Cup a multi-million-dollar operation. When I failed in my attempt to buy my partner's shares, leaving me with a healthy cash settlement and Tom with the company, I was devastated for some time. True, I profited well from the deal. It wasn't an ache in my bank account that troubled me. It was the wound to my pride. Eventually I found peace at a Catholic retreat. When a very wise priest recognized the source of my troubles and reminded me that "a Picasso is always a Picasso no matter who owns it," I was able to do the next right thing and leave my resentment behind me.

If pride is preventing you from doing what you know is necessary to work your way through a crisis, that's easy to understand. It's never about pride alone, however. It always includes the same barrier to handling crises that we encountered earlier: fear. That's what froze an otherwise admirable businessman I'll call Sunil, causing him to avoid dealing with a serious crisis even though he recognized the next right thing to do.

I was told about Sunil by an associate who knew I was searching for examples of personal crises, and who had dealt directly with Sunil. Over the years of their business dealings they had become friends. After his crisis had been resolved, Sunil revealed all that he had undergone during his crisis, and why it had been difficult for him to act.

Sunil's company had been in financial difficulty for some time before the crisis arose, but he avoided dealing with the problem until the day when Pranab, who did the books for Sunil's company, confronted him.

"Pranab was blunt," Sunil told my friend. "He told me that unless I took action my company was two months, maybe less, away from bankruptcy. The bank would not wait for me any longer and my suppliers were at the end of their patience. I had been fooling myself for months and I could fool myself no longer."

The bookkeeper, who was a chartered accountant, reminded Sunil that he stood to lose not only his business but also all of his personal assets. Sunil's importing company, which employed fourteen workers and rented space in a building on the outskirts of the city, was so closely tied to Sunil's personal assets that the collapse of one would trigger the collapse of the other. Sunil had been warned about this danger for some time, but he had chosen to maintain the existing arrangement.

Being forced to face reality was devastating to Sunil. Bankruptcy would destroy his reputation and shatter the pride he took in all he had accomplished since arriving from India as a young man with ambition and little else. In Sunil's mind, it would leave a scar on his psyche that he would never overcome. He and his family would lose their large custom-built home with a swimming pool, the center of the family's social life and the biggest measure of his business success.

Pranab understood Sunil's reluctance to take the necessary steps, but Pranab was a practical man. Besides, it wasn't his pride and reputation at stake here. His job was to deal with facts and, he kept reminding Sunil, the facts dictated that Sunil needed to sell or deeply mortgage his house, apply the equity to the company, liquidate half the inventory in the warehouse at a loss if necessary to generate cash, and lay off about half of his workers. "You need cash," Pranab said. "Lots of cash and you need it quickly. This is the only way to get it."

There was more. Sunil had been a good salesman but a terrible bill collector. Many of his customers were taking three, four, or more months to pay the invoices from Sunil's company, and Sunil had been reluctant to press them for payment. Why? Because most were members of his and his wife's family. Distant relatives in some cases, but Sunil believed they would think less of him if he insisted too strongly on payment. Pranab was not only telling Sunil to collect money on the outstanding invoices but also to take legal action if necessary. And soon.

Pranab didn't stop there. He advised Sunil to withdraw his children from the prestigious and expensive private schools they attended, and dispose of the Florida condominium he and his wife had purchased two years ago. He also warned Sunil about the tax implications they were facing. To settle all the challenges facing him, Sunil would be forced to live in a much more frugal manner for two years, maybe more.

"Unless you can double your sales in the next month and have your customers pay all their invoices within thirty days, you'll be out of money in eight weeks, ten at the most," Pranab lectured Sunil. "You've taken much money out of the business in the last couple of years. Now you have to put some back in."

Sunil believed that Pranab didn't understand his situation. His customers, those to whom he was related by blood or marriage, considered Sunil a partner in their business. His employees were friends. He had even sponsored three of them as immigrants. How could he tell them they no longer had jobs? It was impossible.

"No," Pranab said. "It is necessary." Sunil's family, Pranab suggested, might not even be able to remain in their home if they had difficulty securing an adequate mortgage at a fair rate. They could be forced to move into a rented apartment.

Sunil considered this unacceptable. He could not imagine doing such a thing after all the years of hard work he had invested in his company and in establishing himself as a successful businessman.

"Either you make the tough decisions," Pranab warned him, "or other people, namely the bank, your suppliers, and the company that owns this building, will make them for you."

The acquaintance who told me this story knew about Sunil's background, and understood Sunil's reluctance to face the facts that Pranab laid out for him. Sunil had arrived from India with little more than sheer determination to become a success. It took him years of sixteen-hour days with few vacations or time off, but he made his mark. More than that, he created his identity out of hard work. For Sunil to admit failure would be like giving up everything and returning to India, which was out of the question for him.

Pranab could not force Sunil to do what the accountant knew was necessary. It would be up to Sunil's creditors to do that, and it would be done according to their plans, not Sunil's. When the accountant left Sunil's office, he doubted that Sunil, whom he considered a good and valued friend, would take his advice.

When I heard the story of Sunil and his business problems, I had two reactions. One was to question the decisions that had resulted in the problems he faced. Keeping control of finances and separating business assets from personal assets are two essential parts of running an effective business. It may well have been, in fact, that Sunil was a much better family man than businessman.

All successful businesspeople need to make hard decisions from time to time. If you are unable to make decisions such as ensuring good cash flow and reducing expenses, including the size of your staff payroll when necessary, you shouldn't be operating a business. It's not a matter of greed; it's a matter of survival. If a business fails, all the people counting on it for their income will fail as well.

I suspect that Sunil succeeded in the manner that he did because he was a nice guy, and nice guys are admirable as friends, but they're sometimes (not always) failures as managers and entrepreneurs. And this, I believe, was the barrier preventing him from taking the steps needed to save his company.

He had always been generous with family members. He gave some of them jobs and others made purchases from him. Families are generous and loving with each other. They don't send threatening letters about overdue accounts, or put one another out on the street without a job. They trust and respect each other. What would his and his wife's family think of Sunil if he suddenly insisted they pay up? On top of that, what would the rest of the world think of him if he gave up his luxuries and moved into a rented apartment building just to keep his business afloat? Would they consider him a failure, a loser, someone not worthy of their respect and admiration? He believed he couldn't bear that.

Neither you nor I need to learn more about Sunil's situation to recognize the next right thing for him to do. I suspect he recognized it himself, but he was unable to do it. He found excuses, tried different strategies, and basically denied reality for a month or so until his bank and creditors united to shut down the company and seize its assets.

It was a tragedy for everyone. Most of Sunil's creditors agreed it was unnecessary. Had Sunil taken the steps that Pranab had advised, his company would have survived as a smaller but profitable firm, and over time Sunil, who did not lack basic business skills, could have built the company back to its original size or even have made it larger.

Why didn't he? Because he could not find the peace to make the hard decision—to do the next right thing.

There is great satisfaction in achieving a goal entirely on your own. There is also great risk. When everything is about *you*—*your* vision, *your* energy, *your* glory, and *your* reward—serious problems become *your* fault. Or that's how it seems. Egos are fragile, more fragile than most of us realize. They drive us to success, but when they lie shattered at our feet, they are useless in dealing with crises. As long as you are so focused on caring for your ego that you cannot place your trust in a Higher Power and find the peace you need, you are doomed.

Earlier I noted that encountering a personal crisis is like coming upon a sharp bend in the road that you didn't expect. Perhaps you weren't paying attention, or you forgot to consult a road map, or (keeping up with the times) you didn't believe your

GPS. Either way, by the time you realize what is happening, it's too late to avoid the curve. So what do you do—skid to a stop? Make the turn? Or crash off the road?

One thing you must do is accept that you are not the only occupant of the vehicle. Others are on board with you. They include your family, friends, business associates, and, in Sunil's case, employees. They're along for the ride, but you're the one holding the steering wheel.

Sunil's prime concern had been his own self-esteem. Self-esteem is more than a good thing to possess; it is essential to living a happy and fulfilling life.

Without self-esteem you cannot persuade yourself that you are worthy of whatever happiness you enjoy; thus any happiness that comes your way must be from other sources, such as the gratitude of friends and family. Many people make sacrifices for friends and family with the motivation of basking in their gratitude. Their thanks and appreciation make them feel needed and wanted. If this occurs to you, your self-esteem climbs. You recognize the good feeling you sense is happiness. Happiness feels good, so you continue to act in the same manner, reinforcing your happiness and extending your gifts and sacrifices.

I felt rapport with Sunil and his situation because, as a businessman, I understand how much he put on the line when seeking to build a substantial enterprise. Along with material assets, he risked portions of his identity, including his reputation and his sense of ethics.

I'm writing this after recently resolving a financial crisis myself, one that generated emotional reactions in me similar to those that Sunil experienced.

I had been working for some time on a large project in South America. The project involved building quality affordable housing for the rising middle class in that region. I had acquired the technology needed to get this done from a company I previously managed, and I had discovered the need for such a project through various social organizations I had supported over the years. The project appealed to me on many levels, and I plunged into it wholeheartedly. It represented both an appealing business opportunity for me and a chance to provide attractive affordable housing for people who desperately needed it.

Making the idea a reality would require more than my personal and financial assets. I needed a partner. Together we could attract the other support we would need, and achieve everything I had dreamed of for this particular project.

I thought I had found an ideal partner in a man I'll call Stewart. With an agreement drawn between us, I set off to put everything in place—financing, government support, land acquisition, the works. I was the front man, the guy with the concept and the determination to make it happen. The entire program reflected my vision and my values. So when Stewart, disregarding his word to provide support for the project, announced that he had changed his mind and would not be participating in the development, it reflected badly on me. I had given my word to many people, based in turn on the word of a partner I had trusted. When Stewart withdrew his support—not on the basis of any identified problem but simply because he had changed his mind—the risk to my reputation became obvious. I had made promises that I was now unable to keep. I would be letting down people who had counted on me.

My first reactions to Stewart's breaking of our agreement were predictable. I was disappointed, angry, depressed, frustrated, resentful, and a host of other emotions that blinded me to dealing with the situation effectively. Many of my responses reflected the effect his decision would have on my relationship with business partners in South America whom I had been hoping to assist. If the project vanished, so would my reputation as a trustworthy businessman, my prospects for future work in the region, and a good deal of my pride.

I needed to apply my own solution to the crisis, and I did. I found peace. I took a long walk that relaxed both my body and my mind. During that walk I acknowledged that I had not caused this situation, after all, and the realization of this fact contributed to the serenity I felt. I had no reason to suffer guilt or remorse for my actions. I would survive whatever was to come, and I would do whatever was necessary to correct the situation. But I would neither fret about things now nor worry about how they would evolve in the future. Having found peace, I identified the next right thing to do.

Stewart's support would have included a six-figure cash investment that I was forced to make up from my personal assets, which had already been stretched to the limit.

To put it bluntly, after I fulfilled my promises to others, my family and I were little more than $100 away from being flat broke if things went wrong.

So how did it turn out?

My actions convinced my South American contacts and other potential partners of my commitment to the development, and enabled me to assume Stewart's portion of the project. This left me with a larger share of the company and greater future control over its management. I was better off in many ways without Stewart than I would have been with him.

I make no assurances that events of this kind always work out for the best. No one can. In this instance it worked out for me, however, and my determination to first find peace proved its value once again. When I refused to feel angry and depressed over Stewart's flip-flop on his agreement, and when I trusted a Higher Power to assume responsibility, I found peace. Having found peace, I discovered the next right thing to do. And then I did it.

When we build our happiness on pride alone, we are building a house of cards. And when the house collapses, we face a serious crisis: Our happiness vanishes along with our means of easily regaining it.

Instead of thinking about a house of cards, consider a list of priorities in life that has become legendary among psychologists as a means of measuring our needs as human beings.

Because it represents a structure with a broad base of simple needs rising to a narrowing list of more sophisticated expectations, the list is often referred to as the Maslow Pyramid. It is named for Abraham H. Maslow, the psychologist who introduced the steps in 1943. Maslow didn't present his concept as a pyramid, by the way. Others used the pyramid concept as a means of illustrating the idea and suggesting the upward motion from bare subsistence to ultimate achievement.

So picture a pyramid similar to the ones familiar to us in photographs from Giza, Egypt. The base is built on all our fundamental needs, beginning with air to breathe, water to drink, and food to eat. When we have an adequate supply of these necessities we move up to the next level and seek safety and shelter: a place to sleep, protection from the elements and enemies, and so on.

Safety enables us to rise to the next level on the pyramid. Now we seek love, affection, family, and a sense of belonging to a larger group around us—a tribe, a community, a nation.

Each new level is a step toward the peak, a region Maslow called Self-Actualization, which he defined as the point in life at which you achieve everything you choose to achieve, within your abilities.

Maslow traced the development of humans as social animals, and he was visualizing groups or entire societies, not individuals. But it appears to me that the tip of the pyramid represents more than the end result of moving up from the most basic needs of life through to a point that may be defined as nirvana. I don't believe it has to be that complex, or that each of us must make the climb through all the levels and sublevels suggested by the pyramid. Most of us, of course, achieve at least the middle level of the pyramid, a point where we are loved and feel that we belong, to one extent or another. So the distance from there to the pinnacle isn't as far as it looks.

Maslow's concept struck me as appropriate for this book because it provides a representation of my premise that you cannot emerge from a crisis without first finding peace, trusting a Higher Power, and doing the next right thing.

If you remain buried within the pyramid in the midst of your personal crisis, you can never deal with the situation in a rational and effective manner. Consider three critical levels again: safety … love … and esteem (or self-esteem). In the midst of the crises that were crushing Larry, Jennifer, and Tammy, which of these elements could they find in their lives?

The sudden departure of Larry's wife left Larry feeling not only unloved but also *not worthy* of the kind of love he had treasured with his wife. He felt safe in the relationship that defined who he was, to himself if not to other people, and in the high opinion of his colleagues. Without them his self-esteem dropped close to zero.

Jennifer's love for Benjamin was obviously ill-placed; his abandonment of her was complicated by her fear of losing her parents' love when they learned of her pregnancy, and by her serious consideration of an abortion. To lose both Benjamin and her parents' love, and the safety that she enjoyed within those relationships, would have an impact on her self-esteem similar to the one that Larry felt.

Tammy couldn't feel safe with the end of a romantic relationship, the possible loss of her job, her daughter's drug use, and the risk that she might have to find a new home for both of them. To meet this wave of crises, she would have to draw upon every available quantity of her self-esteem.

All three qualities—safety, the desire for love, and the need for self-esteem—are submerged in the depths of the Maslow Pyramid. Larry, Jennifer, and Tammy have no hope of dealing with their crises effectively until they can rise above those levels long enough to look around and understand their situation.

Maslow didn't name it this way, but I suspect that he would endorse the idea in this context:

*The largest, most important dividend to be enjoyed from achieving Self-Actualization is peace.* Call it "inner peace" if you will, but it still applies. When you rise above the turmoil of striving to achieve all that you believe you need and deserve, and trust in whatever you choose to believe in as a Higher Power, you will find peace. Atop the pyramid, with your eye far from the keyhole that limited your vision, you will see the next right thing to do.

# EIGHT

# Dealing with Finality

*Give sorrow words: the grief that does not speak*
*Whispers the o'er-fraught heart, and bids it break.*
—WILLIAM SHAKESPEARE, *MACBETH*

Not all the crises we confront and deal with enable us to move on with our lives. As we age, we encounter changes that prevent us from restoring the kind of life we believed we enjoyed in the past.

I'm speaking of loss. Not material loss, but the loss of those we love, people who make up not only much of our lives but of ourselves, in many ways. In my experience, the response to the loss of a loved one can be paralyzing to some people because they feel as though they have undergone an amputation. Part of them is gone forever, and they are unable to deal with the loss.

It would be both heartless and useless to suggest to someone who has just lost a family member to death that better times lie ahead. But it is also foolish to assume that the survivor's life is over. Life is to be savored, experienced, enjoyed, and yes, sometimes merely tolerated. It should never be undervalued, especially when others are around to offer love and support.

That's the second tragedy for people like a man I'll call Carlton. Carlton's first tragedy had been the death of his wife, Vanessa, struck by an especially aggressive form of leukemia. Almost before they realized the true seriousness of Vanessa's illness, Vanessa was gone, and two years later Carlton still mourned her passing. His mourning did not involve remembering the happiness they had shared together. In the eyes of his children, he simply refused to move on.

His daughter, Rose, claimed that Carlton still kept all of her mother's clothes. "He won't change a thing in the house," Rose said to a counseling group she hoped to bring him to. "He kisses her picture good night before going to bed. My brother and I never look forward to him visiting us because all he does is talk about Mom. 'I remember when your mother did this,' he says, and 'Nobody will ever cook a roast or sing a song or even sweep the floor like your mother.' Hey, we miss Mom too, but we've gotten on with our lives and Dad hasn't. He's wasting his life, and he's depressing ours."

Carlton's family and friends had given up trying to convince him to build a new life without Vanessa. They had long ago abandoned plans to introduce him to new friends, male or female. Vanessa, they agreed, had been a lovely person, a caring mother, and a good wife, but nothing Carlton or anyone could do would bring her back. They understood this. Carlton refused to accept it, although he claimed he did. "I know she's not coming back," he would say, trying to explain his attitude. "I'm just not ready to move on yet. Every time I think about doing something or going somewhere without Vanessa, I kind of freeze up, and I end up doing nothing. But that's okay. It doesn't bother me. It bothers other people, not me."

One by one, Carlton's friends drifted away. He saw less and less of his son and daughter and their families, including his four grandchildren. "There is nothing else we can do," Rose said to the counseling group. "And it's so sad. My father is only in his mid-fifties and still in good health. He has so much to offer and so many years ahead of him. Now I hear he's being urged to take early retirement by his boss because, frankly, his work isn't as good as it used to be or even as it should be."

Rose feared that without work and sufficient income to maintain his home, her father would continue his emotional decline, leading to economic disaster followed by a major deterioration in his physical condition. She would have liked to care for him as much as possible but with two school-age children of her own and a husband who long ago lost his patience with Carlton ("He has to stop wallowing in his own self-pity and get over it. Just start snapping out of his depression!"), her options were limited.

Carlton refused to label his attitude a crisis. He was simply mourning his loss, and he wished others would understand how much he loved Vanessa. "If they knew what we meant to each other, Vanessa and me," he would say, trying to hold back tears, "they might understand why I act this way."

Rose managed to talk her father into attending a meeting of the counseling group, composed of social workers and survivors.

He refused to add anything to his daughter's description of his actions since Vanessa's death, saying that he preferred to listen for a while. As the meeting wound down, someone asked Carlton what he had absorbed from listening to the stories that others had exchanged through the evening. "I know I need to get past the death of my wife," he said. "And I know that life is for the living. I just don't know how to do it."

Some societies believe that the loss of a life partner ends social activities for the surviving partner. Remarriage and even the exploration of new love relationships are frowned upon. Interestingly, this usually applies to women exclusively, or at least most rigidly. Widows tend to be bound by much tighter restrictions than widowers.

While I respect the traditions of societies other than my own, my identity is with members of North American society and its values, and my concern is for those men and women who, having suffered the loss of their lifetime partners through death, must deal with managing to balance their own lives. How should they behave without the presence of their spouse? How much happiness are they entitled to enjoy? To what extent should they consider the opinions of those who may criticize their actions—especially their efforts to build a new life with another partner?

Those who measure such things report that the death of a spouse ranks highest among all the psychological trauma that occur in our lives. Whether sudden or expected, whether in the midst of a loving relationship or long after the partnership has ended, the impact of a spouse's death is stressful. It is also a turning point—perhaps the most critical one we may experience. It leaves us shaken, unsure, and depressed, and its impact on our ability to reason and conduct our own lives with wisdom can be overwhelming.

Some of Carlton's actions may suggest a mild mental illness that is best addressed by a qualified professional. To some people, the idea that mental illness could be responsible generates an unsympathetic response such as Rose's husband's suggestion that Carlton should "stop wallowing in his own self-pity and get over it."

That's an all-too-familiar answer to many situations that may indicate mental illness. Carlton's son-in-law, I'm certain, would never have suggested that Rose's mother "get over" her leukemia. Carlton did not choose to "wallow" in self-pity. He did it because it gave him comfort. Without Vanessa's presence in his life, he lacked the comfort he had enjoyed for more than half his life. Carlton's actions, such as kissing his wife's picture good night, may appear unusual and perhaps even bizarre, but lacking any reasonable alternative they appear logical to him because they give him comfort.

Carlton could not admit he had a problem, or that he had a crisis on his hands. He dealt with the facts as he understood them. The love of his life was gone, and people in his situation were expected to miss their lost partner. To Carlton this was not a "problem." It was a fact of life, and he responded to it emotionally. How else could he respond? He had suffered an emotional trauma that he had to deal with and he was dealing with it in the only manner he knew: by keeping Vanessa alive in his mind. Calling his sorrow a "problem" would be like calling growing old a problem. Problems can be solved. The only solution to Carlton's "problem" as he saw it would be for Vanessa to return, and that wasn't going to happen. So how could it be a problem?

With that in mind, take your eye from the keyhole for a moment, the same keyhole that Carlton had been looking through for almost two years. And, despite my observation that too many people still belittle mental illness instead of respecting its seriousness, I'm going to stand next to Rose's husband for a paragraph or two.

I don't believe that Carlton was mentally ill, and I suspect that a professional therapist would agree with me. Suffering extended shock from a traumatic event in his life? Of course. But in a state of permanent mental instability? I'm not so sure.

When I look at Carlton's actions, I see a man who desperately desires peace. He is not at peace with either himself or the world around him. Through the keyhole he has been staring into since Vanessa's death, he sees himself as a mourner and the rest of the world as outsiders prepared to criticize rather than support him. How can he be at peace in those circumstances? His only source of peace is to wrap himself in the memories of his married life and find comfort there.

But what if this happened:

What if he could find peace in the knowledge that he and Vanessa loved each other to the moment of her passing, and that the rest of his life is in the hands of a Higher Power who will neither judge his actions nor resent his search for a new happiness? If he could move into that state of mind, and out of the frozen state of mourning in which he found himself, he would know the next right thing to do.

He will not find peace through immediate *action*. It is *peace* he should find immediately, through trust in his Higher Power. The best action for him to take will then follow.

The loss of a loved one represents a major crisis to all of us. Only the duration of the suffering varies. It is not only the loss of companionship and affection, in its various forms, that affects us; it is the removal of a part of ourselves, the amputation I spoke of earlier. That's what generates sorrow, isolation, and fear of continuing our lives without the company of someone who helped fulfill our identity.

We saw proof of this in Carlton's inability to handle the loss of his wife. For a different view, consider Nadia's story, as told to me by someone who had read my book *When All You Have Is Hope*. This person saw Nadia's experience as something of a Shakespearean tragedy, filled with pain and angst.

It had been two months since Nadia's beloved brother Dmytro committed suicide.

Nothing about Dmytro's death made sense to her. He had been bright, handsome, and outgoing. More than that, he had been Nadia's hero. Three years older than her, Dmytro had emigrated from Ukraine with Nadia and their parents when both were young children. Dmytro had guided his sister, his "little pet" he called her, through her first months in school. He taught her the first English phrases she spoke, he defended her from bullies who teased her about her clothes and language, and he was the confidant she needed through her teenage years, when their parents were struggling as immigrants and dealing with their own language, social, and employment issues. The pressure and instability had caused their father to drink excessively, and generated violent arguments between the two parents, drawing the brother and sister more closely together. Now Dmytro was gone.

His note to her, composed moments before he hanged himself in the basement of his rooming house, was both comforting and painful. He wrote:

> *I have hidden my depression from you over all these years because I wanted only happiness for you and did not want to burden you with my problems. Now you are a happy and beautiful young woman while I remain miserable. Please do not see my death as a dark part of your life but as a way for you to be free and happy. Take care of Mother.*
>
> *Love, D.*

Dmytro, Nadia discovered, had been in therapy for some time. Only prescribed medication had controlled his deep bouts of depression. When he insisted that he no longer needed the medication, he spiraled into the dark period that saw him withdraw from family and friends, and eventually even from Nadia, until he viewed suicide as the only means of ending his pain.

Dmytro's request for her to care for their mother was both important and unnecessary. Their father had suffered a debilitating heart attack three years ago. His employer's disability insurance provided a basic income, but caring for him occupied much of their mother's life.

For weeks after her brother's death Nadia's emotions swung back and forth like the pendulum of a clock, except faster and in a wider arc. As much as she felt sadness and despair at Dmytro's death, she remained angry at him as well—angry enough to destroy his suicide note and all the cards, letters, and gifts he had given her over the years. At other times, she awoke from dreams of them as youngsters, when Dmytro was still the big brother who would care for her, and she would be depressed for much of the day.

Her anger at her brother's selfish action grew wider. It had occurred just two months before Nadia was to graduate with her degree in anthropology. She and her boyfriend had agreed to announce their engagement and their plans to marry on their graduation day. It had been a secret that they were excited about revealing. It would also create some much-needed pride in Nadia's parents, neither of whom had completed high school. Dmytro, she was convinced, would have been even more proud of her.

Nadia's boyfriend, Seth, offered to help her deal with her grief, but Dmytro's death continued to haunt her. Nothing made sense anymore, and things that appeared important just a few weeks ago—her graduation, her plans for postgraduate work, her engagement to Seth, her art classes (Nadia's teacher praised her for her natural skill at watercolors)—all seemed silly and empty of meaning.

She was depressed, yes, but it was more than depression that bothered her. She was not suicidal, and she agreed with the advice that others offered. She just wasn't prepared to take it. Not yet.

She knew she had to get past this point in her life. But day after day, she wavered between grief and anger. Some days she refused to leave her room. Lately, she had begun arguing with Seth, heated quarrels in which she would accuse him of outrageous things and question the value of their relationship. In the midst of their last quarrel, which disintegrated into a tearful shouting match, she had come close to telling him that she hated him, and that their wedding plans were off.

She feared she might actually say this in their next angry encounter. And, based on her past actions and current state of mind, she would expect him to agree. She could not bear to lose Seth. Yet she couldn't deal with the reality that Dmytro was gone. Not yet.

All personal crises are unique, even when the causes are similar, as they were with Carlton and Nadia. It's worth exploring other examples of the sort of personal crisis you are undergoing at the moment, primarily to grasp the common means of dealing with them.

For example, if your crisis involves the loss of a loved one, you have every right to the emotions that threaten to overwhelm you. But if you employ your emotions as a means of beating yourself up, or influencing others to change their attitude toward you, you are being destructive at a time when your focus should be on assuming a constructive attitude. Constructive suffering helps you overcome the pain you are feeling; destructive suffering is merely a means of shifting the pain onto the shoulders of others.

Whatever name you may hang on it, suffering of any kind is not a process we need to endure past a certain point in our lives. Both Carlton and Nadia have reached that point. They deserve to live their own lives, and to enjoy their own happiness. They need to find peace, and they need to do the next right thing.

Instead of using *constructive* and *destructive* to define the kind of suffering you may be dealing with, let's call them *existential* and *neurotic*. The words are more precise in their meaning, and they may assist you in finding the peace you need.

Existential suffering is a byproduct of life, and no one can avoid it. We all suffer to various degrees through the process of growing from infant to adult, through the loss of parents and friends, through the range of disappointments and failures that color our lives, and through the inevitable sequence of growing old and facing death. This kind of suffering is best managed through the human spirit, in any manner you choose or that has proven effective for you.

To mourn the loss of a loved one is not merely normal; it is essential. The process acknowledges your own mortality and connects you with others. It also serves to bridge the gap from the event of your loved one's passing to a new phase of your own life. Only against the deep awareness of loss can you fully appreciate life and the happiness available to you.

Neurotic suffering is not a natural part of existence. It is something you create and impose on yourself. Instead of enhancing or clarifying your existence, it impairs your happiness. You may practice neurotic suffering in various ways, such as accepting more than your share of guilt for something, and applying the guilt as a means of punishing yourself and those around you.

In Carlton's case, his suffering was no longer existential; it had become neurotic. Nadia's suffering threatens to become neurotic as well. To deal with the death of her beloved brother, she should be drawing upon her fiancé's strength and support. Instead, she is pushing him away.

Looking into the subject of mourning the death of a partner reveals some generally accepted views on the way people handle such a crisis, especially the differences between men and women. My own experience tends to confirm the fact that men often have a more difficult time dealing with this reality.

Even in this era of accepting and promoting male sensitivity, society continues to impose a burden on men by suggesting they play the role of strong protector in the family. This may or may not be the case in real terms; you and I can both name, I'm sure, relationships in which the woman is at least as emotionally strong and protective as the male. But many men continue to believe it is incumbent on them to stand tall in times of trouble, like some Western-movie sheriff staring down a villain. Women readers may smile at that analogy, but I can assure them it remains true to many men.

This results in a difficulty for some men to display openly the true emotions they feel at the death of a spouse. Women tend to talk freely about their grief to friends, relatives, or counselors, moving through the stages of sorrow and loss and out of their personal crisis. A grieving man is not nearly as likely to do so.

He is often unsure of how he must act. To avoid the prospect of embarrassing himself by revealing his true emotions, he may withdraw from the very people he should be depending upon, and try to deal with his loss in private. He may even, like Carlton, remove himself to some degree from reality, retaining elements of his wife's presence to convince himself that she is not really gone.

The bereaved husband could face another challenge. Many married men have little or no idea of the extent to which their wives manage the household. As long as things are running smoothly, they don't need to know. I am often surprised, given the recent movement away from traditional husband–wife roles, how much of the burden of running a house continues to fall on the wife's shoulders. One study suggests that men perform fewer than 40 percent of household chores.* While women in the study estimated the figure at far less than this, the fact remains that women are responsible for at least 60 percent of all the decisions and actions involving a household. With a wife's death, a man may find that, in the midst of dealing with the traumatic effects of his loss, he must face practical matters he has not encountered before. If the family includes school-age children, the impact on a man suddenly bereft of his wife can be substantially greater.

Carlton does not have to deal with the complexity of school-age children. In the eyes of his daughter, however, he

---

* Oriel Sullivan, "An End to Gender Display Through the Performance of Housework? A Review and Reassessment of the Quantitative Literature Using Insights From the Qualitative Literature," *Journal of Family Theory & Review* (March 2011), pp. 1–13.

needs to find a way out of his sorrow. And while Nadia appears to be emerging from the trauma of her brother's death, she avoids taking steps to get on with her life and seek the happiness she deserves. If challenged directly about the futility of their actions and attitudes, I would wager that both would agree and promise to change things in the future. Maybe tomorrow.

Whatever the nature of your personal crisis, it is too easy to accept that it is unsolvable, or that you will deal with it when you feel stronger. Like tomorrow.

Promising yourself you'll deal with things "tomorrow" isn't just procrastination. It is self-destructive. "Tomorrow" is not the day after today; it is a place where you put things that you don't want to do. "Tomorrow" comforts you and fools you. Ultimately, it can destroy you.

When I was living on the streets of Toronto in my early twenties, I begged passersby for enough spare change to purchase a ninety-nine-cent bottle of wine. I needed the wine to get through the day. The wine would make me feel better and think better.

I believed this with all seriousness. I may have been an alcoholic, but I was not a total fool. I knew alcohol would ultimately destroy me one way or the other, and that the only way I could save myself was to stop drinking. I didn't need a neon sign flashing in front of me all day long, or another guy in the street shouting "Sober up!" at me. I knew what I had to do. So I kept telling myself that I would stop drinking tomorrow, I would get a job tomorrow, and I would escape my situation tomorrow. It was easy to say and even easier to believe, because everyone else on the street panhandling for wine was saying the same thing.

"Tomorrow" even became a joke among us, all my drinking buddies and me. "I thought you said you'd be getting a job today," someone would say to me, and I would reply, "No, I said I would get a job tomorrow. And I will. Tomorrow."

It was only when I began replacing the things I might do tomorrow with the thing that I was growing more and more likely to do, which was die, right there in the street, from stumbling in front of a car or freezing on a winter's night in a back alley, that I recognized I had to do *something*. When I began saying, "I might die like this tomorrow," I was no longer referring to a kind of mental Dumpster where I put the things I knew to be true. This was a real time frame.

I knew that my life was likely to soon end if I didn't change. And when the realization struck me that I *could* change, even if it were just enough to seek the help I needed, I found the first glimmerings of peace. Peace showed me the next right thing to do and I did it. I found the means to tap into the energy of a Higher Power, placing my future in its hands. I have not had a drop of alcohol since that day.

Carlton needs to find peace in his life and in his sorrow. He cannot find it alone while his energy is dedicated to maintaining the illusion that Vanessa is still alive. His children have a role to play. Instead of abandoning their father on the assumption that time heals all wounds, they need to help him pull his view away from the keyhole and find joy, first among his family and eventually in the rest of the world.

Time indeed may heal all wounds, but it does not eliminate all pain. As long as Carlton continues to feel pain he will not find peace, and without peace he will not know the next right thing to do.

Nadia is in greater control of her crisis than Carlton, but she also needs to find peace before moving on. She has lost her beloved brother, but she has a loving relationship with Seth, and this could represent the Higher Power in which she can place her trust. Their love and respect for each other can be a source of security for Nadia, a way for her to find peace. With Seth she may gain a man who respects and loves her in a different but equally important manner.

In the comfort and security she gains from that, she will discover the next right thing to do.

NINE

# Leading Others to the Door

*What you are is what you have been.*
*What you will be is what you do now.*
—BUDDHA

The method I propose for working your way out of the personal crises that are certain to befall you has three positive qualities:

1.  It works.
2.  It is simple to understand and relatively easy to implement.
3.  It can be explained to others, and you can assist others to use it for their own crisis situations.

You value the people in your life because they give your own life meaning. Solitude is a wonderful thing from time to time.

I often crave solitude to meditate, to reflect on my life, and to recharge my batteries. But solitude isn't a way of life; it is an interval between the events of your life. Most of us prefer interacting with and assisting people we know who need our wisdom and support. We instinctively want to help friends through difficult periods in their lives, and assisting them to find peace may be the most practical step we can take in building our own sense of self-worth.

That's the attitude of Cathy, a woman who told me of her friend Sarah. Both lived in Toronto, but at opposite ends of the city.

"Sarah and I have been friends since high school," Cathy explained. "We didn't see each other as often as we might have liked, but we'd call or email back and forth, and we'd be sure to get together at Christmas, on birthdays, and so on."

They were brought together recently by an email from Sarah, asking if she and Cathy could meet after work one day.

After they'd exchanged quick hugs and ordered glasses of wine, Cathy asked what was bothering Sarah.

"She said, 'Everything,'" Cathy explained. Sarah believed she and her husband, Joe, were drifting apart. He had never been very demonstrative, but lately they appeared to have nothing to say to each other except grumbles about the behavior of their children, Jay and Kylie. Jay was always sullen and Kylie had a snappish sarcastic attitude that Sarah could not abide. And then there was work.

"Sarah told me she was always being bypassed for promotions that she knew she deserved," Cathy said. "The most recent had been the second one so far this year. With almost twenty years' service with her company, less two years off for maternity leave, Sarah claimed to have all the credentials necessary to fill the position, plus consistently positive job-ratings credentials. Everyone she consulted agreed she was more than qualified to handle the divisional manager position, yet two weeks earlier it had been awarded to a man nearly ten years younger than her."

Just to rub it in, Sarah told Cathy, she had trained the new divisional manager when he first arrived ten years ago. "I showed him the ropes myself, turned him into a good manager, let him lean on my shoulder when he had problems," she said, the tears beginning to flow. "And now he's going to be my boss!"

Sarah admitted that, on some mornings before going into the office, she sat in her car in the parking lot and cried, turning her head so that others wouldn't see her tears. She had wanted the divisional manager position not just for the prestige and satisfaction it would offer her, but for the things that she and Joe needed to get their lives back in order.

In Sarah's opinion, her children were almost out of control. They didn't relate to her and her husband. They were no longer part of the family that Sarah had dreamed of having, and had worked hard to bring together. They were two individuals, off in their own world. "They don't relate to either of us anymore," Sarah said of Jay and Kylie. "We need to bring them back into the kind of family we used to have, where we did things together. We don't do *anything* together anymore."

To Cathy's surprise, Sarah believed the answer was for her and Joe to buy a cottage—invest in a weekend retreat, perhaps near a lake somewhere. It would be a place where they could bond like a family again, the way it was a few years ago when the children wanted to be with their parents, when they enjoyed their parents' company, just hanging out. With a cottage, they would go swimming and fishing in summer, cross-country skiing and snowmobiling in winter. Kylie and Jay could bring their friends along. The cottage would help bind them as a family. Sarah's parents had had a cottage when Sarah was a child and it had been the center of the family's activities.

Had she earned the promotion to divisional manager, Sarah believed, she and Joe would have been able to afford a cottage. If they purchased a cottage and winterized it, the place could have become their retirement home. Sarah had always dreamed of retiring in the country. It seemed so idyllic. Now it appeared impossible. She had not received the promotion. She would probably never get promoted. What was the use of planning and dreaming?

By the time their meal arrived, Sarah's sadness had been replaced with anger that threatened to boil over. "Those bastards on the thirty-eighth floor took a dream from me when they gave the divisional manager job to a guy who didn't even know where the washrooms were until I showed him," she told Cathy. "I practically held his hand for the first year while he figured out what our business was all about, and what do I get for being nice? A stab in the back!"

Management had deprived Sarah and her family of many things by giving the job she deserved not just to a man, but to a *younger* man! "How do you fight that?" Sarah asked, and before Cathy could reply, Sarah said, "You don't. You can't fight it. I've been fighting things like this for years and I'm tired of fighting, tired of losing, tired of it all."

Cathy reached across the table to enclose Sarah's hand in her own, and she held it while her friend calmed down. When Cathy asked Sarah if it was helping her to talk about her situation, Sarah nodded, smiled, and gathered herself together. Cathy told her to keep talking, and what she heard next was shocking and yet not surprising.

Two days earlier, Sarah told Cathy, she had sat in her car for almost thirty minutes after work, feeling helpless and depressed. She finally drove home to an empty house. Joe was at his biweekly poker game, Kylie was working a shift at the fast-food restaurant where she had been hired two weeks ago, and Jay was at basketball practice. With no appetite for dinner, Sarah curled up on the sofa and tried to sleep. Instead of sleeping she recalled a cousin who had committed suicide when Sarah was in her teens. She tried to remember how her cousin had done it and wondered what it would be like.

At the sight of Cathy's alarmed expression, Sarah assured her that she wasn't seriously considering suicide. She was, however, imagining something else.

What if she found somebody who could understand what she was going through at work and in her marriage? It wouldn't be Joe, who seemed happy to plod along at his accountant job, playing golf and poker with his buddies, and falling asleep on the sofa after dinner.

She began toying with a fantasy, and fantasies always made her feel better. This fantasy involved another regional manager, a guy named Jordan, whose office was just down the hall from her own. Jordan was a nice guy who often told Sarah jokes to make her laugh. He dressed well, too. She liked a guy who knew what to wear to make himself look his best.

Cathy asked if Jordan was married. "I already knew the answer somehow," Cathy told me.

Sarah admitted he was married, but at the moment this didn't matter. It was just a fantasy, after all. Sarah needed someone to pay attention to her and to understand her frustration over her career. Jordan would know what Sarah was going through in ways that Joe would never understand. Besides, nothing had happened, although Jordan was always suggesting they get together and have a drink after work someday. The next time he suggested it, Sarah intended to take him up on the idea.

"What do you think that will lead to?" Cathy asked.

Sarah had looked away before answering, in a voice that sounded more than a little defensive, "If it makes me feel better about myself, I don't really care."

Not all the challenges we face in life arrive with red neon signs flashing: CRISIS! CRISIS! Not all of them make us feel bad, either. Sometimes the early stage of an impending crisis is attractive in various ways. If I were to have a glass of whiskey or a beer, I expect it would taste very good to me. It would also launch a major crisis in my life, and shatter my years of avoiding alcohol. In Sarah's case, the fantasy of a fling with a man who claims to understand her at a time when she believes she needs understanding represents a crisis situation.

Sarah is rationalizing the idea of taking a step that could

ruin her marriage and seriously damage her relationship with her children. She is not just on the brink of a crisis; she is practically in the middle of one.

We shouldn't try to seize the high moral ground when it comes to judging Sarah. The root of her dilemma isn't a desire to have an affair. It is a number of other things, including her experiences at work, her disillusion with her marriage, and her changing relationship with her children. Which one of these is cause and which is effect? Does Sarah's dissatisfaction with her family life emphasize her anger with her employer, or vice versa? Does she see a potential affair with Jordan as a solution, or is she using her dissatisfaction with life as an excuse to have a fling?

It doesn't matter. Sarah is at a crisis point in her life. She is hurt, she is angry, she feels helpless, and she may be on the brink of making a decision that could threaten her happiness and her family's future in ways she cannot predict.

Without knowing the answer to the cause-or-effect question, we can at least deal with some assumed realities:

*Joe doesn't pay Sarah as much attention he did when they were married eighteen years ago.* It's a fact of life: romance changes with time. Sometimes it deepens, and sometimes it fades. Sometimes it changes in other ways without altering the affection one partner feels for the other. We may have little control over these changes, but we have total control over our reactions to them.

*Sarah's daughter, Kylie, is difficult, and her son, Jay, is sullen.* Is there a problem here? Aren't they behaving like 90 percent of teenagers? Has this really reached a crisis point?

*Would the actions of her husband and children disturb her as much if she were more satisfied with her career?* Sarah believes she is the victim of sexism and ageism, and she may well be correct. Society in general has yet to catch up to its commitment to equality between men and women in the workplace and elsewhere, and managers exist who favor the energy and promise of youth over the wisdom and stability of experience. We can cut Sarah some slack on this point. Or there may be other reasons for the apparent plateau of her career. After all, Sarah has yet to discuss her situation in detail with her supervisor.

This is not meant to belittle Sarah's feelings. Her pain and confusion are real and may be justified. But Sarah has her eye fixed on the keyhole, and it is only through the keyhole's limited vision that she sees the world, including her employer and her family, conspiring to prevent her from finding the happiness she rightly deserves.

Cathy was correct to be concerned about Sarah and the decision Sarah was about to make. But what could Cathy do at the moment? What would *you* have done?

It is difficult to evaluate from a moral position Sarah's imminent decision to seek solace in someone besides her husband and friends, and I don't intend to do it here. For one thing, only Sarah can measure the desperation she is feeling. More than one social observer has claimed that the act of adultery is a cry for help. This seems to have a good deal of truth to it when seen from an objective viewpoint. In Sarah's case it appears to be true.

Whatever Sarah's motivation may be in entertaining the idea of an affair with Jordan, she is already in a crisis situation, based on our definition of the term. She finds her work situation intolerable, her family life stressful and unsatisfying and, if she fulfills her fantasy with her coworker, she will alter her marriage in a way that can never be completely repaired.

One of the things that Sarah appears to be doing, although I suspect she would deny it with lots of conviction, is transferring her pain from herself to her family. Sound unlikely? Think of it this way: If Sarah follows through on her fantasy of having an affair with Jordan, she will in one way or another punish Joe for his inattention to her, and punish her children for blocking her from their world. I'm no Freudian psychologist, but I suspect there is more than a grain of truth to this idea. It also fits my earlier premise: *In the midst of a personal crisis, our minds do not operate in a rational manner.* Whether you choose to believe Sarah's imminent decision to seek comfort with another man is rational or irrational is your call. I believe it is not only an irrational move but also one that, despite its appeal on both physical and emotional levels, could lead to long-term problems that Sarah cannot see coming.

As a close friend, and as someone with a good deal of understanding of Sarah and her dilemma, Cathy faces a crisis of her own. Does she attempt to persuade Sarah of the foolishness of having a fling with Jordan, pointing out that it won't solve the problems that are driving her there and will surely create new and more serious challenges? Or does she stand back and let her lifelong friend perhaps walk away from a marriage that Cathy had always felt was good and worthwhile?

When you are in the midst of a personal crisis that shakes your world, it also threatens perhaps the most valuable asset you own at the moment—your relationship with family and friends. Those who love and care for you are affected indirectly by the same pain and fears that affect you. They want to help—they are often desperate to help—but feel as unable to cope with your situation as you do. Platitudes and promises of better days seem empty, and any advice they may offer sounds unqualified.

Cathy feels this way about Sarah's situation. So, in a very different context, do the children and friends of Yuri, another individual I heard from as a result of my book *When All You Have Is Hope*.

Yuri understood about death. He had spent most of his working life in the medical field and had watched his parents pass away, his father after battling cancer for more than a year and his mother as a result of congenital heart failure.

But the sudden, unexpected death of Yuri's wife, Susan, struck him with a force he could not handle. She died overnight, having fallen asleep on a sofa in the den after dinner. "She had a headache," Yuri told his friends when they gathered at the suburban home where Yuri and Susan had raised their three children. His chin quivered as he spoke and his eyes began flooding with tears. "I thought it was nothing, and brought her a couple of aspirin. When she told me they weren't helping and the pain was growing worse, I assumed it was a migraine so I suggested she turn out the light and close the door. That's the way I had been told to deal with a migraine. Darkness and—" He began to break down. "Darkness and silence."

At ten o'clock, their normal bedtime, Yuri peeked into the den and assumed Susan was sleeping, so he tiptoed into the bedroom and quickly fell asleep. Only when he awoke a few hours later and realized that Susan was not beside him did he discover she had died of a massive stroke.

Susan's passing dealt Yuri a double blow. They had been a part of each other's lives for almost forty years, and had looked forward to a retirement filled with travel and visiting friends and relatives located across the country and in Slovakia, where Yuri and his parents had emigrated from when he was a young boy. Those dreams would never be fulfilled. And as much as his family, his friends, and his colleagues in the medical field tried to wipe away his feelings of guilt, he continued to blame himself for her death. Had he paid more attention to Sue's symptoms, he might have spotted signs of an oncoming stroke, or even responded with a call for treatment that may have saved Susan's life.

"I mean," he said tearfully to his son, Cameron, "there I was, sleeping soundly in bed and she was dying a few feet away. I'll never get over it. Never ..."

After Susan's funeral, Cameron approached two of his father's oldest friends, asking for help. "Dad still has so much to give and so much to live for," Cameron said. "Can you help me bring him through this crisis?"

"What can we do?" the friends asked.

Cameron replied that he didn't know, beyond expressing their sorrow. "But there has to be more someone can do to help my dad," he almost pleaded. "Isn't there?"

Easy answers in life are less common than most people realize. And easy answers in dealing with a personal crisis created by the death or serious illness of a loved one are even more rare.

Once again, the root of the pain you may suffer, beyond the bereavement process and yet still a part of it, is fear—fear of a future without the presence of someone you regarded as your life partner. So how do you handle it, either as someone who has lost his or her partner or as people like Yuri's family members and friends who want to guide him through this crisis?

It's about clarity. It's about finding the point where you see clearly the decisions you need to make, and are able to get on with a life that is headed in a new direction. That's what you need in the midst of a personal crisis, and the people you love and care about need the same thing. So what can you do to assist them to find peace and do the next right thing? You might consider Job.

The story of Job is one of the most familiar tales in the Bible. It's also the most confusing to many people, but at least one appropriate lesson comes out of it.

To refresh your memory:

Job may have been the wealthiest man of his time. Several scholars consider the Book of Job to be among the oldest in the Bible, so the measure of his wealth should be seen in context. We're told that he has seven sons and three daughters. He owns seven thousand sheep, three thousand camels, five hundred yoke of oxen, and five hundred donkeys, and has a large number of servants.

All of this is taken from him for no reason that he knows or can understand. With his children, servants, and livestock gone, his body begins to erupt in painful boils, which is enough for him to begin asking, in effect, "Why me??!!" As far as he knows, he has lived a virtuous life. True, he has amassed a lot of wealth, but he believes he has done so through his own efforts and has no reason to feel guilty of wrongdoing.

In the midst of his personal crisis, three friends arrive to console him or at least to listen to his complaints. When Job claims that he has lived a moral life, one friend suggests he must be wrong. "Truly righteous people are never made to suffer this way," the friend suggests. "Only the wicked are tormented like this, so you must have done something terrible." His two other "friends" agree, one suggesting that things could be worse; Job is being punished by God, who is merciful. "Obviously you're not being punished as much as you deserve, because 'mercy' means treating a person better than that person deserves," Job is advised.

Job doesn't buy that argument, demanding that his friends point out any evil he has committed, and claiming with some justification that his behavior has been no worse than that of his friends. So why is he suffering agony while they are not? Why are their children and livestock healthy, and their bodies free from boils? Eventually a younger and more compassionate acquaintance of Job disputes the arguments of the first friends, Job's troubles begin to vanish, he gains a new wife and family, and lives to be a hundred and forty years old.


Job's friends may have been sincere in their efforts to help him, although from this perspective of time and religious values let's say they were less than encouraging. Their ideas were based not on Job's particular situation but on their own inflexible thinking processes. Job needed help from his friends, but not that kind of help. Help from true friends who had undergone their own personal crises, along with professional counsel via therapy and perhaps medication, would have been invaluable to Job. And you should not withhold any practical assistance you can offer. It's important, however, to do and say the correct things, and avoid doing and saying the things that Job's friends offered. Here is a list of don'ts to remember when assisting friends in a crisis:

*Don't say "I understand."* You cannot fully understand the inner turmoil of someone enduring a serious personal crisis. Even if you experienced a similar event in the past, your response and your pain were unique to you. You may have acquired wisdom in knowing how to deal with the situation, and you should be prepared to offer it at the ideal time. But telling someone that you fully understand their current state of mind is not helpful to them.

*Don't suggest the person is overreacting.* I am amazed when I hear someone advise another person in crisis to "Snap out of it!" or "Suck it up!" It's admittedly more a male than a female response, but it is hurtful no matter who delivers the command. When the target of such a tactless command cannot snap out of it or suck it up, he or she will feel inadequate or angry or both.

I know a woman whose beloved older sister was suffering from terminal cancer. When a friend asked why she appeared so glum, the woman described her sister's illness. "Get used to it," her friend answered. "My brother died last year. At our age these things are just going to happen." Her statement was true, and she may have been trying to suggest gathering courage and facing reality, or some other means of dealing with the situation. But it was also shockingly insensitive. Try as she might, the woman whose sister was dying could never feel the same toward her friend. Over time the friendship dissolved.

*Don't offer advice.* In the midst of a personal crisis, the last thing anyone needs is unsolicited advice. People need only assistance in finding peace, and an opportunity to identify the next right thing to do.

Understanding what not to do is helpful, but when you're dedicated to helping a friend or loved one move through a crisis period by finding peace and doing the next right thing, you want positive guides.

You can tailor your reaction according to your relationship with the person you're seeking to help. Consider starting with the approach I use when one of my daughters is having difficulty dealing with something that has happened, or has not happened, in her life. What do I need to do?

First, I need to assure her that I am there, and that I care about her feelings. The best way to do this is to follow my instincts as a parent: Give her a hug and listen to her problem. Hugs are a natural human response that anyone can use whether the relationship involves a child, a parent, or a friend. Even men, I might add. A sincere hug, along with someone who will listen closely to a problem, are two entries to peace.

After listening to my daughter's problem, my response is "How can I help?" Then I wait for the answer. Frequently, especially with teenagers, you will be informed that you cannot help, that the problem is too big or too complex or beyond your ability to solve it. Things tend to be different with adults. In an adult world there is always something you can do to help. It is often logistical—assisting with a memorial service, informing relatives, drafting an obituary or résumé, even doing the laundry or the grocery shopping. Each bit of assistance brings the person you are helping closer to finding peace, and having found peace they will recognize the next right thing to do.

If, in either case, you are told there is nothing you can do to help, your next question is "How do you want things to be?" In cases of the death or abandonment of a spouse, the answer may be an impossible task: "I want my wife/husband/child back." Expressing these impossible goals aloud validates the impossibility and unlikelihood of them becoming reality, so you repeat the question "What can I do to help?" The question is worth repeating because it focuses the mind on something besides the problem. You can always do something to help, and you have helped simply by asking the question.

The actions and decisions you choose through life shape you. They define who you are and what you become, and for the most part these decisions and actions are yours to make and take.

This doesn't mean you are in total control of your life at all times. The world may bump against you with its own selfish needs and its sometimes innocent acts, causing you to react in one way or another. And you make decisions. Sometimes your decisions are made without any awareness of the harm they may cause yourself and those around you. Sometimes you know exactly what their impact will be.

No matter what personal crises befall you, somehow and somewhere you likely helped them to happen. A critical step in dealing with crises is to admit this is true.

It's difficult, I know, to acknowledge this fact when you are lost in the effects of a crisis. It may feel like kicking yourself while you're down. But it's not. In fact, it's the first step in reaching to help yourself back onto your feet again.

It would be easy for me, for example, to blame my alcoholism on the various abuses I suffered during my teenage years. Sexual abuse plus the inability of my parents to provide the comfort and support I needed to deal with my trauma helped justify my craving for alcohol. If I chose to, I could excuse much of my behavior and most of my problems by blaming others in this manner:

> *My alcoholism wasn't my fault. It was the fault of my parents, who were cold and aloof. It was the fault of the sexual abuse I suffered from figures such as the priests and policeman, who should have been models of authority and moral standards. It was the fault of the people who sold me beer and wine, even though I was obviously a teenager and often already drunk. It was the fault of the cops who chose not to press serious charges when they found me drunk behind the wheel of a car, and of the social services who offered no assistance to get me off the street and into a rehab program, and on and on.*

My fault? How could my situation be my fault? I was only a kid. Later I became a victim. Then I was homeless, a street person with a serious alcohol problem. None of this changed until I shifted from those identities into the only one that really counted: I was someone who first found peace, and then found his way out of the train wreck that had been his life.

One word I did not use in proposing that you assist others in overcoming their personal crises is *karma*. I avoided it not because I don't buy the concept—in fact I do, wholeheartedly—but because the word has been tossed around so indiscriminately in Western culture that its definition has become diluted. If I ask some people how they define karma, they are likely to respond with "What goes around comes around." Perhaps, but that's like saying gravity is the force that will kill you when you jump off a mountain. There are other aspects to consider.

The early Hindu and Buddhist philosophers defined karma not as punishment or retribution but as an expression or consequence of natural acts. In fact, the word itself means *deed* or *act*, in a context similar to Newton's third law of motion, usually described as: *To every action there is an equal and opposite reaction.* Karma is not fate. Fate suggests that everything is preordained and ignores free will. We possess free will that can mitigate or neutralize the effects of fate, and the effects will always be there for us to enjoy or suffer according to our actions. Speaking for myself, I'll choose joy over suffering every time.

Call it karma if you wish. Call it a means of self-healing if you prefer. But one way to find peace, and to begin to emerge from your crisis, is to assist others in their troubles. Of course, you should be prepared to offer your assistance to friends whenever you feel they need it. But I remain deeply impressed by the value of assisting other people in their emotional turmoil as a means of dealing with my own challenges. I can always find both the energy and the alternatives to assist others, even when, for the moment, the same energy choices are unavailable to me for my own needs.

There are various explanations for this. One suggests that you use the problems of others to divert your attention from your own problems, but I find that a little mechanical, if true to some extent. Another interpretation is to assume that it feels good to help others, and if offering your assistance in that manner deadens some of your own emotional pain, it's worthwhile. Okay, but here's a more clear explanation as I see it:

The mind cannot feel two deeply contrasting emotions at the same time. You can't be simultaneously depressed and happy. I don't know of any single act that provides us with more meaningful joy than helping others and basking in their gratitude and shared happiness. So once you have absorbed, tested, and confirmed the lessons and techniques in this book, make them available to those whom you love and care for when they are in need. You will heal yourself in more ways than you may know.

# TEN

# Step One:
# Find Peace by Turning Away
# from the Crisis

*More people change by feeling the heat*
*than by seeing the light.*
—ANONYMOUS

I don't know if I stumbled upon the concept of reversing the path that my instincts suggested, the one that dictated I would only find peace by first solving the pain of my personal crisis, or if I thought the idea through logically, like some sort of philosophical puzzle. I only know what I have learned, what I have applied through much of my life, and what I have done to assist others in dealing with their personal crises. I also know that it works.

The process does not require a guide, a video tutorial, an operator's manual, or an app on your smartphone. It needs you to take three simple steps that you could, if need be, connect into one mental action:

1. Find peace.
2. Trust a Higher Power.
3. Do the next right thing.

Let's begin with the first step. The proverb about there being nothing new under the sun is appropriate when dealing with the personal crises you will encounter through your life. Being told that countless numbers of other people are facing similar pain, disappointment, and fear of the future may not be reassuring, but it is true.

This doesn't change the seriousness of the situation or the misery it may be causing you. It's *your* crisis and *your* pain, and knowing that others may be in similar straits does not provide much practical assistance. It can, however, offer assurance that, having dealt with problems much like your own, others have emerged safely. Like Allison, who was resigned to the fact that her marriage of twelve years was about to end.

Allison and Anwar had begun, like most young couples, with golden dreams that for many years they appeared to fulfill. Their first child, a son, arrived three years into their marriage, followed by a daughter two years later. When Allison decided to give up her teaching job to become a stay-home mother until their children were enrolled full-time in school, Anwar's career at the engineering firm began to take off. He was quickly promoted into a managerial position and fast-tracked for a future partner-ship, removing much of their financial strain. They were able to obtain a mortgage on an almost-new suburban home in a good neighborhood, take winter vacations with the children, and enjoy the prospects of a bright future.

Two years ago, Allison began noticing changes in their relationship. Anwar's work involved more travel, later hours, and frequent weekend assignments. When she questioned the time he spent away from home, he grew defensive. He also became dismissive of her opinions and prone to explosions of anger. She began suspecting him of hiding a relationship with a female colleague at work, suspicions confirmed when she found receipts for gifts she had not received and hotel stays she knew nothing about. When she confronted Anwar he admitted the affair, said it had been only a fling, and told her it was over. He also accused Allison of "sneaking through my private notes like a thief," and refused to visit a marriage counselor.

She soon learned he had not ended the affair, nor did he give any hint that he planned to take whatever steps would be necessary to save their marriage. Her dreams destroyed, along with the affection and closeness she knew they had once felt for each other, Allison was ready to do what was necessary to preserve happiness for herself, resolve the insecurity their children were feeling, and perform the break as quickly and as painlessly as possible.

Allison suspected that Anwar was not keen to end the marriage. It would make him appear as the villain, a role she knew he detested. The owners of his company were rather moralistic, and would not look favorably on the dissolution of his marriage, especially if they learned the circumstances. It would surely influence their decision to make him a partner of the company, an ambition Anwar had held since he joined the firm.

Everything appeared to rest on Allison's shoulders. The situation with Anwar was intolerable, but making the decision to start divorce proceedings was distressing. Before consulting a lawyer, she needed to know she would be doing the right thing. More than that, she needed to know *how* to do the right thing.

If Allison has done everything in her power to save her marriage and maintain security and happiness not just for herself but for her children, she must choose either to take control of an untenable situation or play the role of a doormat for as long as her husband chooses to remain within the family. This is an easy decision: No one should be a doormat to anyone in any situation.

The barrier that Allison faces in getting on with her life—in doing the next right thing—is her concern about making the right decision. She wants total assurance that her decision to end the marriage is 100 percent correct.

Life isn't like that, of course. Decisions made where others are involved, especially when the others are children, are never easy and never perfectly correct. They are only obvious and necessary.

The prospect of enduring a failed marriage is almost by definition (Who can ignore the word "failed"?) traumatic. Like all traumas, it floods the mind, leaving little room for other emotions. Everything Allison considers over the next few days will be both colored and dimmed by the expectation that the dreams she harbored for years when marrying Anwar are shattered. She expects to face many things, all of them painful: loss, loneliness, embarrassment, and humiliation. In that frame of mind, how can she find peace and prepare herself to do the next right thing?

The truth is, she can't. She needs an interim stage between the shock of her realization and the serenity she desperately requires. How can she do it? By overcoming her fear of what she believes is about to happen. And fear always comes from one place: the unknowable future.

The only view of the future that you have is the one you create in your own mind. For some people, this view is wonderfully warm and bright to the point of being idealistic. For other people, especially in the midst of a personal crisis, the view may be depressingly dark and essentially hopeless. Neither is more real or more likely than the other.

Among the wisest advice you are likely to hear about dealing with life is to take it one day at a time. Almost everyone can understand this concept and its importance in finding happiness, but few people grasp how to practice it. You are often too busy worrying about what may happen next year, next month, or tomorrow to live within all the pleasures available today. In the middle of an unanticipated crisis, fear can grow enormously. Compounding the fear is the knowledge that you can do little, if anything, to control the threats. You begin playing the game of What If?, and all of the "ifs" are bad. You find yourself paralyzed by fear.

This doesn't mean that you should discard your visions and plans for the future. When I was thirteen years old, I read about the legendary developer William Zeckendorf and all that he had managed to achieve by first visualizing what he wanted to do, then taking the steps to do it. Through years of alcoholic haze from that point forward, I retained Zeckendorf's ideas and valued them as a goal worth pursuing, and this was responsible to a large degree for my eventual business successes. Many of the things I have achieved in business were made possible because I held on to the vision of Zeckendorf's success and grew determined to emulate it. I visualized the future, but I did not *live* in it.

Contrast this with Allison. Lost within all her fears and other emotions, she is living in a future filled with uncertainty. She needs to find peace. There is no fear to be experienced when we are at peace. And there is no route to peace as long as we are crippled by fear.

I know one man who, when his marriage dissolved in the sudden and unexpected departure of his wife, became emotionally paralyzed, unable to work or relate to family and friends. For several weeks he became a recluse and seriously contemplated suicide. It took more than a year for him to overcome not the depression that so many people assumed had engulfed him, but the fear he felt.

"My identity, my success, my happiness had all been based on that relationship," he explained. "When it vanished, so did all those other elements in my life, and I feared what would become of me. I didn't want to work, I didn't want to see anybody, and I couldn't stand my own company."

Eventually he rose out of his darkness, his fear of the future. It took a couple of challenging years but eventually he met a woman vastly different from his former wife, the one whom he believed had been responsible for his happiness. He soon realized that this woman provided strengths that he had never enjoyed in his previous marriage. His friends and family revealed their affection and enthusiasm for the woman, and within six months of their first meeting they were married. That was almost twenty years ago, and the marriage has grown more solid and fulfilling with each year.

"After my former wife left," the man said, "I believed I would never find anyone who made me as happy. Well, in a way I was right. I found someone who made me *more* happy."

Cynics may call this rationalization, but his friends agree that he is sincerely happier now than in his earlier marriage. My point in telling this tale—you may know of one that is similar—is to show that fear of the future is a waste of time and energy. We do not know what the future holds, and in the middle of all the angst we're suffering during a personal crisis, the most dominant emotion we have is fear. It prevents us from finding the peace we need to move forward.

I am currently in a stable and fulfilling marriage, but as I detailed in *When All You Have Is Hope*, it is not my only experience with marriage.

Shortly after lifting myself both out of the gutter and away from my dependence on alcohol, I met a lovely young woman named Joanne. She understood the complications of alcoholism; we met when she was helping an uncle who had been trying to overcome his own alcohol addiction through the support of the same counseling group I was using. This made it easier for her to accept the difficulties I faced.

I needed and valued Joanne's presence in my life because I

had been both smug about my achievement at no longer being a slave to alcohol and concerned about my ability to walk the straight and narrow path of sobriety for the rest of my life. Joanne, I believed, would help celebrate my achievement in overcoming alcoholism and assist me in maintaining it.

Soon we began talking of a permanent commitment, and Joanne invited me to meet her parents in Montreal. That's when complications developed. I quickly realized they were a well-to-do and socially prominent family whose status was well above my own middle-class background. This was more of a problem for me than for them. They not only approved of our relationship, but encouraged us to become husband and wife, believing we would be good for each other.

I can't fully explain the influence that Joanne's family had on my decision to marry her. Joanne had her own reasons to marry, but mine included using her family ties as a means of resolving issues with my parents. After suffering through my teenage years, in which I managed to destroy several of my parents' cars and a good deal of their happiness and security, my father and mother had written me off. With good reason. For the sake of the family, including my sister and brothers, they insisted I leave the house. They went further; they wanted me to leave Montreal and move out of the province. That's how I found myself stumbling in an alcoholic haze through the gutters of Toronto.

Hearing of my situation in Toronto, my family was hardly surprised. What else could they expect of me? We didn't stay in touch. The only telephone call they likely expected to receive concerning me would have been an announcement that I had died, probably in a gutter while clinging to a wine bottle.

Instead, they were stunned to hear me announce that I was sober, employed, and engaged to the daughter of one of Montreal's most eminent families. It was unfolding like the ultimate rags-to-riches fairy tale. Instead of standing on street corners with an outstretched hand, I would be moving among the highest social circles in the country, as far from the gutter-dwellers of Toronto as from the moons of Jupiter. How could I resist making the decision to marry Joanne? An enchanted future was waiting for me to walk into it, my lovely young bride on my arm, facing comfort, security, and respect. Especially respect.

Some people warned me that I was moving too fast, too soon. It was impossible, they said, to turn my life around as quickly as I had without carrying immense amounts of baggage into the marriage and placing it on someone else's shoulders. I refused to believe them. All I could see was the magical fairy tale. All I wanted was the promise of living happily ever after.

We were married in an elaborate ceremony celebrated in the presence of some of the most prominent members of Montreal society, as well as my own doubting parents.

The fairy tale lasted barely six months. Despite our efforts, Joanne was unable to accept the man I had been, and I resented her inability to fully appreciate what I had achieved. We began the final argument with angry words and ended it in sullen silence. The silence was broken forever when, after fleeing back to her parents' home, she telephoned me to say the marriage was over.

More than twenty years later, when I was getting a lot of press coverage as a result of my business success and charitable activities, I received a letter from Joanne suggesting we get together for a chat. With some nervousness I agreed to meet for coffee. She greeted me warmly, and I was delighted to learn she had a career as a psychotherapist who appeared frequently as a guest on various radio and TV shows dealing with marital relationships. She was also the proud mother of a lovely daughter.

Our short meeting was more than enjoyable. It was deeply rewarding, because it made me realize that although I may have behaved like a cad all those years ago, I had provided Joanne with some joy while we were together. In fact, as we shook hands while saying good-bye, she smiled and said, "You know something, Frank? I'm glad I married you."

My decision to marry Joanne had not been "pure" in the sense that it promised and delivered equal amounts of happiness and security for both of us. And Joanne's decision to end the marriage was far less than ideal, because I learned during the meeting that our divorce sent her into a spiral of depression she took some time to overcome. On the positive side, it inspired her to launch her career as a therapist.

The experience of seeing Joanne and exchanging the ways in which each of us had found happiness provided me with a new tactic in dealing with personal crises. I cannot ensure that it will work effectively for you, but having grappled with and defeated many other crises in my life using this tactic, I want to share it with you now.

Whenever I take the three steps that represent the core of this book's message—find peace, trust a Higher Power, and do the next right thing—I assume the viewpoint of watching a realistic and unpredictable action movie for the first time. "I wonder," I say to myself after I have done the next right thing and am waiting for events to develop, "how all of this is going to work out." Sometimes the ending is expected, and sometimes it is a surprise. Sometimes the result is costly in one form or another, and sometimes, as with the case of Joanne, it is soothing and reassuring.

Either way, I am fully prepared to accept and deal with whatever evolves from my choice. The resolution neither frightens nor overwhelms me. I have done the next right thing, and I know that no other option would have been guaranteed to produce a better result.

Remember my earlier story of the man who was devastated when his marriage ended abruptly because he feared he would never be as happy again, only to realize three years later after he remarried that he was actually happier? It brings to mind an idea that a wise man proposed many years ago. He suggested that once we feel we are doing the right thing, the forces of the universe come to help us somehow.

I have found this to be true. If it appears mystical to you, and if you would prefer a more intellectual explanation, consider this:

As long as you are pursuing something that is neither in your own best interest nor in the best interest of others, you stand with your eye at the keyhole, often while doing things that you know are not morally or legally correct, or are not in your best interests. This also explains why you always know what the next right thing to do is once you step away from the keyhole, even when you discover that the next right thing often is the most difficult step to take. This makes sense. Only sociopaths find it easy to do the *wrong* thing. To do the wrong thing means focusing on the negative and ignoring messages from your conscience to do the *right* thing. As long as you limit your vision to the view through the keyhole, you are blind to the better alternatives available.

I believe in the concept of unleashing the forces of the universe in my favor whenever I choose the next right thing. It supports my personal concept of a Higher Power. If you choose a more intellectual explanation for finding peace within yourself, that's fine too. Like the man who was happier in his second marriage because he believed he was married to a better woman than in his first marriage, it doesn't matter whether he was rationalizing it or whether it could be proven to be true. Only one thing mattered: He was happy and content, and his pain was gone. It was not important how he arrived at that place—only that he got there safely.

Back to Allison.

As difficult as it may be for her to imagine, she needs to walk away, in her mind, from the current situation. She can do this by refusing to inject herself into the future. Yes, she can and must make plans—about dealing with divorce, if that is the inevitable outcome; about searching for assistance in handling the legal and financial aspects of no longer being married; about assisting her children as they encounter their own personal crises when their parents separate; and about grappling with other issues that are likely to arise.

Walking away does not mean she is giving up on her marriage, although most people would agree she would be

justified in doing so. It means that she needs tc
of her own happiness, and taking steps to recove
do this while trapped within the manipulations
and the emotional turmoil they are causing her. Sl
peace, and within that peace the next right thir
apparent. She will also discover, I am sure, the nec
to do what must be done.

One thing she must cease doing is living in t
inevitable unrealized fears of the future are paraly:
the legendary deer in the headlights, she is froz(
terrible situation whether you are in the path of {
truck or in the midst of a personal crisis. You don't n
at a time like this; you need movement towarc
peace.

Allison needs to believe only that the future wil
than the present, given her husband's actions and
needs to train herself to assess and treasure each day
and to find reasons to look forward to tomorrow. Sl
remove herself from the trauma she is experiencing.

She needs to find peace, and she can find it \
knowing that she is basically a good person who has bee
by someone lacking her positive qualities. Reminding
this fact—that she has behaved admirably in compai
her husband, supported by the awareness that she ha:
right to happiness as Anwar, may represent the first st(
the peace she needs. It will not make her feel good imn
nor should she expect it to. She needs only to take that
and claim possession of it. Her next step may be to glo:
love and affection of her children, and perhaps in anti

e pleasure of teaching, if she chooses to return to it in Anwar's
sence.

Small steps, yes. But together they lead toward peace, which
where Allison needs to be.

# ELEVEN

# Step Two:
# Draw on a Higher Power

*Space is as nothing to spirit;*
*The deed is outdone by the doing.*
—RICHARD REALF, *INDIRECTION*, 1864

The biggest challenge that most people will have in implementing the ideas in this book is accepting the existence of a Higher Power and trusting in it to find the peace they need. I have addressed this point throughout the book, emphasizing that we can locate a Higher Power if we open up our minds to its existence.

I find the peace I need from my own concept of a Higher Power. Sometimes it is easy to locate; sometimes it is more difficult and challenging. But it always appears.

If, despite your efforts, you are unable to grasp the existence of a Higher Power as a means of finding peace, ponder this notion:

*We are not human beings having a spiritual experience; we are spiritual beings having a human experience.*

Or consider the crisis facing Brenda, a story told to me by another reader of *When All You Have Is Hope*:

At age thirty-one, Brenda was ready to die. She believed she had been ready to die for ten years.

In high school, Brenda became addicted first to alcohol and later to prescription drugs, paid for with sex or with money stolen from her mother's purse. Her middle-class parents provided all the material benefits Brenda needed, but only minimal emotional support. They believed that their church, where they insisted Brenda join them and her younger sister each Sunday, would satisfy those needs.

"I went to church with them almost every Sunday, even into my high school years," Brenda said. "Sometimes I was stoned. I would be falling asleep while listening to a sermon about how much God loves me. My parents would ground me when they caught me sleeping, even before they knew it was because of the drugs I was taking. Being grounded after church didn't bother me because it meant I could sleep for the rest of the day."

Brenda grew confused as she grew older. She had found comfort in her religion as a younger child and sought it as a teenager, even while depending heavily on drugs, and somehow this didn't seem right. Wasn't her religion supposed to provide comfort and security? If this was true, why did she keep taking drugs? But maybe it wasn't so bad. After all, there was nothing in the Bible that said God didn't want you to take drugs.

In her final year of high school, Brenda became pregnant. Her parents, distressed and angry, insisted she marry the father, who was her drug supplier. When he balked at the idea, her parents gathered evidence of his drug dealing and threatened to turn it over to the police. He gave in. After the civil ceremony, Brenda and her husband found an apartment in an old house. He began working at a long series of menial jobs to support them, and continued to deal drugs. When he angrily prevented Brenda from attending church on Sundays or religious holidays, she avoided raising the idea with him again. Within three months of the birth of her first child Brenda became pregnant again. Following the arrival of their second child, her husband began beating her and calling her ugly, useless, and stupid. At age twenty-four she swallowed as many drugs as she could find in their home and woke up three days later in an intensive-care unit.

"I felt worse than I had before I took the pills," she said. "I was a failure again. I couldn't even take my own life!"

Things grew worse. Social services took the children away for several weeks until they felt confident that Brenda could become a capable mother. Brenda's parents, who had provided money and gifts for the children while urging Brenda to return to church with them, withdrew further. The beatings from her husband resumed.

Brenda's only concern was for her children. Her attempt at suicide, she realized, had been selfish. She promised she would remain alive until her children were six and seven, old enough to remember her when they were adults. "On my daughter's sixth birthday," she promised herself, "I will kill myself and end my pain."

Three months before that day, Brenda's pain turned to anger. Not at her parents, not at her abusive husband, not even at herself. She was angry at God. "All those years I went to church as a child," she said, "I tried to be good. I prayed every night, and even when I went to church stoned, I still believed in Him. I knew I had done things wrong, like stealing money and being with boys just to get drugs, but I thought I would be forgiven. I thought as long as I believed in God I could trust Him to help me. Now nobody's helping me. Well, I promised myself I would do something. I just hope I have the courage to do it right this time. But I'm scared. I don't know what I am scared of most. Killing myself as I promised, or not having the guts to do it."

Saying those words aloud—changing a thought into action, or at least into plans to take action—had an immediate sobering effect on her. She loved her children. She couldn't bear to have them hurt, as she had been, and she knew her death would hurt them. But she was hurting as well. So what could she do?

People have had crises of the spirit for as long as they have believed in a Higher Power. Every prophet and religious leader has endured them, and most emerged from the crisis stronger.

Brenda's crisis is not a spiritual one, however. It is a different kind of crisis, one that cries out for assistance from a source she seems incapable of reaching.

The primary challenge at the moment is to prevent Brenda from fulfilling her promise to commit suicide as a means of ending her pain and humiliation. Her threat is not empty. She has already attempted suicide, and many people who make one attempt repeat it until they succeed.

You may feel Brenda is supremely selfish in considering suicide while responsible for the care of her children. This only indicates the degree of pain she is suffering, and the extreme measures the pain is tempting her to consider. The question of Brenda considering suicide should not be a moral judgment on our part; Brenda is already susceptible to moral judgments from others. She does not need another.

Brenda has been let down by everyone and everything she should be able to count on. Her parents, her husband, and various social services have not been capable of providing Brenda with the assistance she requires. So where can she turn? To a Higher Power, someone or something that can transcend the challenges of her life and relieve the agony she suffers.

That's the textbook answer. But where is the reality for a woman who has every reason to reject the idea of seeking help through God? And what of the millions of people in the world, some of whom I fervently hope will read this book, who either have difficulty dealing with or reject outright the concept of God?

I face this challenge each time I discuss doing the next right thing. It's neither my job nor my intention to change people's attitude toward the existence of God. I merely want to assist them in overcoming challenges they face in dealing with whatever personal crisis they are undergoing.

My response, whenever someone cannot help but equate a Higher Power with the concept of God, is to suggest what God is *not*. God is not a religion, God is not a church, God is not a place, God is not a set of rules, and God is not dogma of any sort.

This makes it difficult for many devoutly religious people to embrace the concept of a Higher Power as a means of finding the next right thing to do. Their fixed image or definition of God or some other deity brings expectations and formalities that get in the way of trusting the Higher Power to resolve the personal crisis. Those who identify with any religion are almost by definition constrained by it.

My Roman Catholic upbringing included total acceptance of rituals and doctrine that represented the foundation of the faith—the Eucharist, confession, the Stations of the Cross, and on and on. I am not being critical of either the rituals or the Church that professed them—only that they are by nature rigid, and rigidity is not what you need to assist you past your crisis. You need assurance that, without either restrictions or expectations, a power exists to envelop you in trust and carry you forward. Like the third man in Geiger's book, it is there for you to rely upon, and you need no more specific description or confirmation than that.

So it does not matter to me, or to the success of the technique I am proposing, whether you believe in God or not. If you practice a formal religion, nothing in any legitimate system of faith will object to you finding a moral means of ending your fear and discomfort. Set the dogma aside and open your mind to a more nebulous presence, one that defies definition beyond its own existence.

Even such loosely defined power remains inaccessible to some people. If you consider yourself among them and find any concept of a Higher Power challenging, consider the suggestion that each of us has a higher purpose within ourself. Not a Higher Power, a higher purpose.

You are not a single-cell creature unable to see beyond the biological necessities of surviving and reproducing. You recognize purposes that extend beyond your identities as a living creature. These purposes may be things you do for others and for yourself, and they define you as a human being. You have a purpose when you seek food and shelter. You have a higher purpose when you do the same for others.

Your higher purpose may be to serve as a good parent to your children, showing them the love, comfort, and joy they will carry to the generation that follows them. It could be to assist others who need your help ... to fulfill a job or objective that will return material benefits to yourself and others ... or to interpret and beautify the world through music, literature, art, or another means of expression. It can be any of a dozen different goals. All are purposes beyond the objective of simply remaining alive. If you have higher purposes, does it not follow that you can acknowledge the presence of a Higher Power? Otherwise, what drives you to serve a higher purpose?

Some people who reject the traditional concept of God accept the power of the universe because it suits their perception of reality. They cannot grasp the concept of a God of the Old Testament or a similar deity from another religion, but they understand the forces of nature that dictate the behavior of planets and galaxies. To them, this is a much Higher Power than any they can conceive on their own. That's fine with me. Whatever name, face, or identity you attach to your Higher Power, it exists to assure you that you are not alone.

Neither, you will recall, were the explorers and adventurers mentioned in chapter 4. When they found themselves facing death in harsh and unforgiving environments, and desperately needing strength to survive, they felt the presence of a Higher Power. The apparent presence of someone else, guiding and encouraging them and providing comfort and strength, occurs too often to dismiss it as a pure figment of the imagination. Charles Lindbergh told of the presence of friendly beings aboard the aircraft he piloted as the first person to fly solo across the Atlantic, and noted climber Reinhold Messner, in his book *The Naked Mountain*, described the risky descent with his brother Gunther down the over four-thousand-yard face of an ice-clad mountain. The descent was foolhardy but necessary to save their lives, and it was made more dangerous because Gunther was severely weakened and ill. At one point the brothers seemed doomed, until:

> *Suddenly there was a third climber next to me. He was descending with us, keeping a regular distance a little to my right and a few steps behind me, just out of my field of vision. I could not see the figure and still maintain my concentration but I was certain there was someone there. I could sense his presence; I needed no proof.* *

And in case you believe that these apparitions appear only to physically active people under extreme stress, consider the

---

* Reinhold Messner. *The Naked Mountain* (The Mountaineers Books, 2003), p. 229.

tale told by Vincent Lam in the foreword to John Geiger's book *The Third Man Factor*. Lam is a busy and fully qualified medical professional (and a fine writer—his book *Bloodletting and Miraculous Cures* won the Giller Prize as best Canadian novel in 2006) who told of a visit from a third man while he was in the midst of studying for medical school entrance examinations. In contrast with other events from Geiger's book, Lam encountered his third man while taking a shower in an attempt to relieve the enormous stress he felt. He also referred to the presence as an angel:

> *The angel spoke to me and gave me advice. It offered practical suggestions on how to conduct my daily life, how to learn, and how to manage my emotions. The angel did not promise admission to medical school, but assured me that things would work out as they should ...*
>
> *I decided to record some of this practical advice. I got out of the shower, sat down at the computer and wrote several pages of guidance that was directly dictated by the angel's voice. I saved those words on both the hard drive and a floppy disc, went to bed, and had my first restful sleep in weeks.* \*

Lam easily passed his entrance exam, launching an exceptional career in medicine.

---

\* Vincent Lam in the foreword to John Geiger, *The Third Man Factor: The Secret to Survival in Extreme Environments* (Penguin Canada, 2009), p. xiv.

*The only requisite for a Higher Power is that it be greater than you.* If you choose, you can assign qualities to it such as being loving and caring. It is your choice; it is your power. Some may assume the Higher Power is nature itself. Others may portray it as consciousness, existential freedom, the force of creation, or the entire universe. Names are equally subjective. One individual using a self-help program that required placing trust in a Higher Power labeled his "Grandfather," which seems perfectly appropriate. Another chose to think of the Higher Power as a good boss, and he would wake each morning thinking, "Okay, boss, what've you got for me today?" I don't know any sympathetic member of the clergy, in any faith, who could seriously object to this means of finding solace in your belief.

The concept of placing yourself in the hands of a Higher Power is simply an admission that you cannot handle your current crisis all by yourself. That's a given; if you could handle all the challenges thrown at you during a personal crisis, you wouldn't need anything to assist you, including this book. Sympathetic friends and family members may support you in their own way, but *they cannot make the changes within you that are essential at this time.* To navigate the shoals of your situation, it is going to take more than you and your support group alone. It is going to take your own concept of a Higher Power.

Holding an image or identity of a Higher Power in your mind provides another benefit: You have a target for your prayers. If the word *prayer* makes you uncomfortable, think of it as a petition. You need something. What's more, you deserve it. The ability to provide what you both need and deserve exists in a power that can provide the comfort, wisdom, and strength necessary to handle the crisis you are confronting. Why not submit a petition? It needs only one name: yours.

Wherever your concept of power resides—in heaven, in a church, in a synagogue, in a temple, in a mosque, or within your heart—locate and use it when you need it.

If you accept the premise of God, you have many options for using this as a source of the Higher Power you need, and it is not necessary to communicate your needs in a formal manner. Sometimes it's better to make it as direct and even as colloquial as possible, a means of avoiding the fixed creeds associated with formal religions. Like the woman in the next story.

A therapist once described a woman under his treatment as suffering the effects of an experience very much like Brenda's. The woman had led a life somewhat more in line with the teachings of her religion than Brenda, faithfully attending church and abiding by the Ten Commandments, yet she still had suffered betrayal and cruelty from family, friends, and employer. In her forties she despaired to the therapist about her life, and about how her religion had failed to protect her from suffering.

"You're angry at God," the therapist suggested, and the woman replied that yes, she was very angry at Him. All of her devotion, sacrifices, and prayers had apparently meant nothing. Didn't she have a right to be angry? Wasn't she justified in asking, maybe even demanding, that He explain what she had done wrong? Or maybe what *He* had done wrong?

"So ask Him now," the therapist said. "First, tell Him about all the suffering you are going through, then ask if this is fair reward for keeping the faith and obeying all the laws you had been instructed to obey."

The woman felt self-conscious. It seemed foolish to her. She would, after all, be talking to empty air. "We can change that," the therapist said, and he placed a chair in front of her. "Imagine He is sitting in this chair, facing you," the therapist said. "It will make it easier to hold a conversation."

And it did. Cautious at first, the woman grew more confident and noticeably more angry as she spoke. "I have not been fairly treated," she said. "All my life, from the days when I was a little child, I believed in you and I believed in my church. More than that, I insisted that my husband share my belief and he did, and we raised our children to believe in and obey you, and they did." She went on for some time, growing more emotional each minute until her eyes were filled with tears, her fists were clenched, and her anger became almost palpable. When she ran out of words she lowered her face into her hands and sat crying softly, waiting to regain her composure.

When she had settled down, the therapist asked the woman to sit in the chair she had spoken to, the one she imagined had been occupied by God. He suggested she respond, as God, to her expressed complaints. "God," the therapist said when the woman had exchanged chairs, "this woman is angry with you. She has just spent a good deal of time detailing all the ways you have let her down. Now it's your turn. What can you tell her?"

Without hesitation, the woman, speaking as God, said in a voice as loud and dominating as any she might imagine God owning, "*I want you to seize your freedom!*" Then she sat back and, with a look of contentment on her face, she smiled. When the therapist asked what she was feeling at that moment, she replied, "Peace."

The woman had expressed what her own spirit was demanding, but she had to become God, for a moment at least, to speak it aloud and heed the wisdom. She not only placed her trust in her particular Higher Power. She also employed it as a means of breaking free from the burden she had been carrying, and of finding the peace she needed to do the next right thing.

# TWELVE

# Step Three:
# Do the Next Right Thing
# (You Always Know What It Is)

*Our deepest fear is not that we are inadequate.*
*Our deepest fear is that we are powerful beyond measure.*
*It is our light, not our darkness, that most frightens us.*
—MARIANNE WILLIAMSON, *A RETURN TO LOVE*

The crises you face in life almost always involve people and how you respond to their actions. You may encounter crises encompassing your finances, your legal situation, and your security, but the biggest challenge you face when dealing with crises involves your response and the response of those around you.

That's why the true-life stories of Larry, Jennifer, Sarah, and the others demonstrate the challenge we face in search of the peace we need during times of crisis. Here's another demonstration, involving a man named Lowell:

The collapse of Lowell's marriage represented a deep personal crisis to him. No surprise there. Except that he and his wife, Evelyn, had recently become "empty nesters," with two of their three children working at good jobs and their third in her last year at university. Lowell's small marketing company had been doing well, but he had planned to begin stepping away from its day-to-day operations, leaving him more time to pursue his hobby of restoring classic cars.

Things hadn't been perfect between Evelyn and him for some time, but he blamed this on the long hours he maintained at work and his evenings spent rebuilding cars in his garage. Less time at the office would restore things with Evelyn, Lowell believed.

One Sunday afternoon, Evelyn went into the garage to tell Lowell she was visiting her sister across town, and would be back by dinner. Lowell grunted something in acknowledgment and returned to working on his vintage car.

When Evelyn returned two hours later she announced to Lowell that she "had to leave."

Lowell had no idea what she meant. Leave where?

"I'm going to live with my sister," she said. "I need to. For a while."

When Evelyn offered no further explanation, Lowell staggered through his surprise and began asking his friends and his children if they understood what she meant, and why she was leaving "for a while." That's when he discovered that Evelyn had been having an affair for several months with a family friend, a man Lowell played golf with from time to time. His friend had been widowed the previous year, and Evelyn's initial expressions of sympathy to him had turned into something else. She could no longer continue hiding her unfaithfulness to her husband. Her constant lies and excuses had created the migraine headaches she had been suffering lately. She had decided to move in with her lover, but feared telling Lowell directly.

Lowell was stunned by not just these revelations but by his own blindness and stupidity. Discussing it with his children offered little consolation. They sympathized, but did little more. Their loyalties were divided between their two parents, and their attention remained focused on their own lives and concerns. When Lowell discovered they had known of their mother's affair and chosen not to tell their father, assuming it would "burn itself out," he cut off all contact with them, saying he could never trust them again.

Lowell began to spiral into depression. He gave up golf to avoid encountering his former friend and former wife at the club, sold his business and his antique cars, moved into a small apartment, and began a series of counseling sessions.

"I'm no longer brokenhearted," he confessed to a friend. "I got over that. My therapist says I'm not as crazy as I thought I was. Just depressed and traumatized. I don't like what I am or where I am, but I'm stuck in this situation. I can't trust anybody anymore. I miss my kids, but they sided with their mother against me. How can I go to them now? I can't. I've got my pride."

His friend asked what Lowell was going to do for the rest of his life.

"I don't know," Lowell replied. "Sometimes I worry, and sometimes I don't care."

Was he depressed?

"Not according to my therapist," Lowell replied. "He doesn't think medication will help and he says I'm basically sane. I guess that's good news. He just tells me to get on with my life, and I am. It's just not the life I wanted."

Lowell's most revealing comment about his situation is to confess that he is "stuck" in it. It's clear that he doesn't like it, and would prefer to start forging some new life. He also would like to renew his relationship with his children. But he can't.

He could begin by calling his children. They may not, after all, have "sided" with their mother but simply tried to remain neutral. Taking the initiative to call them sounds easy unless you are Lowell, who appears to have lost trust in them and in people generally. Therapy helped him past the serious mental state he found himself in after Evelyn left, but now he needs to help himself, and he can't.

He is clearly not at peace and he obviously cannot remove his eye from the keyhole. In this case, the keyhole is limiting more than his view of his situation; it is limiting the time frame he is locked within. He insists on looking only at the past because, while it brought sadness and loss into his life, it is not frightening like the future.

Lowell's means of finding peace and relying on a Higher Power are probably no different from those in other examples I covered earlier. No one can define his Higher Power for Lowell, although I suspect it may be the love his children have for him, if he can be convinced of its existence. In any case, we know the next right thing for Lowell to do. It is to renew his relationships with his children and friends, and begin to heal the wounds that he keeps open and bleeding. Why does he keep them open?

Maybe because the pain feels reassuring. Sometimes it's better to feel discomfort than to feel nothing at all. And sometimes wounds begin to heal whether we want them to or not.

Lowell's therapist has confirmed that he is not mentally unstable to the point of requiring medication, but he is clearly unhappy with his life, and is unable to make the changes needed. It's Lowell's emotional state of mind that is locking him into a situation he neither sought nor is able to control.

While Lowell's crisis is the direct result of an emotional shock due to the actions of his wife, Evelyn, other crises are the product of cold, calculated business decisions. Supposedly there is nothing personal about these kinds of actions. Movies such as *Wall Street* and *The Godfather* ("It's not personal—it's business …") illustrate this in dramatic Hollywood fashion. Responses to these kinds of crises, however, are always born of emotions and personal values. Sometimes both.

Several years ago I was involved in the launching and management of a company in the medical services industry. Our business plan was better than good—it was terrific. We needed, however, to build the operations quickly and establish a dominant position before others stole our thunder. Accelerated growth meant locating sources of cash and negotiating with major investors. It also would involve franchising as a means of moving into a large number of markets in a short period of time.

Franchising I knew, thanks to my experience with Second

Cup, where I had managed the franchising side of the business. I needed specialized help, however, with the investment side of things, and hired a man with experience in locating investment funds and promoting the opportunities our company would generate. Let's call him Charlie. I didn't know Charlie, who had built his success in another region of the country, but he came with an impressive résumé and a record of financial management that met our needs. He drove a hard bargain, but we agreed to bring him on board as a partner.

It soon became evident that Charlie had the contacts and skills to attract the cash we needed to expand. Thanks to Charlie's efforts the company grew as we had hoped and Charlie, whose contract included transferring a large number of the company's shares to his name, prospered as much as the rest of us. The expansion was gratifying, and our strategy proved to be right on target. We began moving too fast for competitors to block our growth significantly. Charlie was, in effect, driving the bus and the bus was speeding along the route we had planned.

But there was a problem. The more I looked into the way Charlie was raising funds and structuring our financial setup, the less pleased I became. Charlie did not appear to be doing anything illegal, but his approach just didn't match my ethical standards. Each time I questioned a move Charlie made to attract funds from investors, I was told in so many words to mind my own business and leave the details to him.

I was torn. On the one hand, I was involved in a rapidly growing company providing an essential service to an enormous market at an attractive price. We were creating good jobs for many people who needed them, and attractive future prospects for investors and franchisees, all of it largely as a result of my initiative. I took a lot of satisfaction from what I had achieved, as did most of the team I had assembled.

On the other hand, accepting everything that Charlie was doing put me in conflict with my principles, and this proved emotionally draining. A direct confrontation with Charlie risked ending his association with the firm and the potential launch of legal action by him, which would halt the company's growth as we had plotted it.

Time passed, and no matter how much I tried without launching a direct confrontation, I could not get Charlie to change his tactics. At the same time, I could not alter my standards or dispel my discomfort over some of the things Charlie was doing. One day I admitted to myself that I was in the middle of a crisis. Something had to change, and it would be either my system of values or my relationship with the company. I took a pause in my work to seek advice from those familiar with what was happening, and listened carefully to them and to my conscience. Both confirmed my feelings.

I ceased evaluating the losses I would suffer by enforcing my own code of conduct, and stopped considering all the things that the company's success might have enabled Nancy and me to enjoy. When I did this, I found peace. When I found peace, I instantly knew the next right thing to do.

Keeping my cool and eliminating any personal references where Charlie was concerned, I told him I could no longer be a part of the company if he continued to operate it the way he had been doing.

Charlie's reaction was just as I expected. He told me that he was, in effect, waging a war, and that we needed to seize the high ground in competition with our "enemies," meaning existing and potential competitors. We could do this by using every weapon at our disposal, or we could do it by being "nice guys," acting more like Boy Scouts than U.S. Marines. He chose the Marines. Nice guys, he reminded me, finish last, and there was no way he was going to let our company finish anywhere but first.

Having anticipated this response, I informed him that I was prepared to divide our respective assets and walk away from the firm I had helped launch.

Charlie was shocked. He had been doing nothing illegal, he reminded me, and I agreed with him. Legally, his actions were acceptable to the courts. Morally, they were offensive to me, and I wanted out.

Charlie called me a fool. Did I know how much money I was leaving on the table if I left? Did I have any idea what the company would be worth in the future if I supported him? Was I crazy to give up this once-in-a-lifetime opportunity?

I wasn't crazy. In fact, having announced my decision to Charlie, I felt more contented with things than I had been for quite a while. I realized that acknowledging the crisis over Charlie and his actions, and choosing to do something about it, was the best decision I had made for some time.

We divided the assets of the company. In Charlie's mind, he did much better than I did. I wanted things settled quickly and cleanly, so I walked away with less money than I might have, had I negotiated more aggressively or remained in place for another year or so. Charlie continued running the company in the same manner as before. Eventually one of the competitors grew larger and overtook the company, and Charlie was forced to sell the firm.

Charlie did well, but I did better. Charlie pocketed more money, but I held on to my ethical standard. I have no idea what an ethical standard is worth, but it is worth substantially more, in my mind, than the money I might have made had I tolerated Charlie's methods of doing business.

The contrast between my experience with Charlie and the crisis faced by Lowell is significant. Lowell views himself as someone who has lost a battle that he didn't know was occurring. His apparent indifference to his wife's needs and happiness cost him a relationship that had been the source of much of his identity. In my case, I knew about the conflict I was engaged in, because it was raging within me. My decision cost me more money than I have dared to add up, yet by another measure the price was less than Lowell paid.

The thing that unites Lowell and me represents the core of my message:

*In any crisis situation there is always the next right thing to do.* I remind you once again: *You always know what the next right thing is.* You may not admit it to yourself easily because the next right thing is often the most difficult thing to accomplish. That's what makes it hard to accept. When you are suffering the kind of pain that Lowell, Krystal, Larry, Jennifer, and others endured, you naturally don't want to hear about choosing the most difficult option available. You just want the damn pain to go away!

*It goes away when you find peace.* And you always find peace when you put your crisis in the hands, the care, the qualities, the comfort—however you wish to describe it—of a Higher Power. You need the Higher Power to carry the load, to get it literally off your back so you can stand up straight and start moving again.

That's when the next right thing to do appears not only obvious but easy.

# A Few Parting Words

Throughout this book, I have focused on the means of dealing with personal crises. I did this because I know how important it is for people to find a path leading out of the hell of their crisis into the heaven of a new place, with the promise of new rewards and new pleasures. The change from old to new is rarely easy, often painful, and always significant.

"Do the next right thing" is an after-the-fact response strategy. The anecdotal examples and guidelines I related in this book concern events that have already occurred in people's lives, as opposed to events that should have been foreseen and avoided. Most personal crises arrive in our lives unbidden and unforeseeable. This presents a conundrum because, in the midst of an event that distorts our perspective and weakens our resolve, we are expected to view things clearly and to act with supreme logic.

This sounds to me like advising people how to survive an automobile accident like this: "Here is what you do while trapped in the wreckage of your car while checking to see how many of your limbs are still attached and functioning." Surely it is more important to learn how to avoid an automobile accident than survive one. With skill and luck, many people can go through their lives without encountering a serious auto accident, but you cannot be expected to avoid encountering personal crises that are the result of the death of a parent, the end of a relationship, the loss of a job, the onset of a serious illness, or some similar incident. These are absolute crises, as we saw in chapter 3. While they cannot be avoided entirely, we can prepare for them with the confidence that we will understand how to deal with them when they occur. Admittedly, experience helps. You don't need to have a serious car accident to learn how to avoid one, but having survived a personal crisis prepares you to cushion the impact of the next one.

Conditional crises, resulting from your own actions and decisions, are no less upsetting and serious, but they bring clear and immediate direction for the next right thing to do. It's always easier to know what to fix when you were the one who broke it in the first place.


One of the most effective ways to avoid or deal with personal crises is to elevate the joy you get out of living. Crises seem to occur most often to people who view life as a chore to be completed, not as an adventure to be experienced. This is more than an observation; I believe it is rooted in the idea that the challenges we face in life are found more in the way we respond to events than in the events themselves. If you encounter a rude or unhelpful clerk in a store, you cannot change his or her actions as you walk away fuming. You are completely free—and well-advised—not to waste energy on mulling over your reaction to the treatment because *this is the only part of the event that you control.* You can't go back and change the experience, and I'm sure that little you can do will make the clerk a warmer and more helpful individual in the future. Yet many people will permit such a small incident to color the rest of their day and even beyond.

Compared with the kinds of crises I have covered in this book, dealing with rude clerks represents (or should) barely a ripple in your day. The basic lesson remains appropriate, however: Handling events tossed at you by life in a positive manner, as opposed to viewing every setback as a disaster, makes you better equipped to deal with them more successfully.

Some people may sneer at this idea and suggest that anyone who greets life's challenges this way is a Pollyanna. In case you're not familiar with the term, "Pollyanna" refers to Pollyanna Whittier, the main character in a 1913 children's book. Living with a stern, humorless aunt, Pollyanna is always looking for a reason to be happy no matter what occurs in her life. She focuses on things that bring her happiness, such as knowing that a golden sun shines behind black clouds; because of this, her name has become representative of anyone who seems to remain naïvely cheerful even in a difficult situation.

You may become aware of your inadequacies in the midst of your crisis, but naïveté is probably not one of them. As long as you assume that the crisis will end badly, or that it will simply continue ruling your life like some perpetual soap opera, you won't be in a position to move from the old to the new. You will never find total peace. You will never remove your eye from the keyhole. You will never recognize the next right thing to do.

It's not Pollyanna-ish to search for the good things that may arise when you decide to accept the change resulting from your crisis. But we can all find examples of times when the change from the old to the new led to a better outcome, including:

- the abandoned husband who eventually met and wed another woman who, both he and his friends acknowledge, made him happier in many ways than the wife whose betrayal he had mourned for some time
- the suddenly widowed woman who would always miss her husband and mourn his passing, but who discovered talents in art and education she never knew existed and now had the freedom to explore them
- the frustrated executive who walked away from his job to avoid the office politics he hated, and who launched a business that brought him more time to spend with his family and more income than the job that had produced only ulcers for many years.

The best way to move from the old to the new is to focus upon the things that you *expect* to be better, that you *hope* to be better, and that you *insist* will be better. That's not being Pollyanna. That's being someone who refuses to be a victim of circumstances. So how do you label someone who tackles each challenge in the same way despite experiencing the same failure each time? Is *crazy* too strong a word?

Sociologists studying the effects of personal crises on individuals have discovered that people open to the lessons of experience are best able to meet adversity through "a philosophical reorientation and a new direction in life plans."* Carve your way through that academic language and it sounds suspiciously like doing the next right thing, doesn't it?

The biggest barrier to doing the next right thing may be that you've muddled your way through previous personal crises during your life, often with a less than satisfactory outcome, and decided you had made the best of a bad situation. Even when looking back at the crises you may have handled with success, I'll wager you invested a good deal of time and suffered a fair amount of pain to overcome them. And each time you came across another crisis of whatever nature, I expect your response was to endure its effect in the same manner. If I may use the term in a colloquial rather than an academic sense, that kind of action is *insane*.

Over the past few years, a new definition of insanity has crept into our language. In place of *unsoundness of mind*, or a similar phrase that did the job in my parents' generation, we now hear that a symptom of insanity consists of repeating the same act over and over, and expecting to get a different result.

---

* Richard G. Tedeschi and Lawrence G. Calhoun, "The Posttraumatic Growth Inventory: Measuring the Positive Legacy of Trauma." *Journal of Traumatic Stress* (July 1996), pp. 455–71.

The description works because it's dynamic. We can imagine someone repeating an obviously foolish act over and over, saying "This time, it'll be different," and of course it isn't. Whether this qualifies for a true definition of insanity or not, I leave to professionals to decide. Is a man or woman who marries five or six times, believing each time that he or she has finally discovered permanent happiness without changing the actions that destroyed the earlier relationship, truly insane? Or is there a more accurate and palatable description? I can't think of one.

We all believe we can change for the better. And we do from time to time. But we will never change as long as we put off doing it until tomorrow.

When I was living as an alcoholic on the streets of Toronto, focused only on begging enough money for that day's bottle of wine, I repeated the same act over and over. It involved telling myself, every day, that I would change tomorrow. "Let me just get enough alcohol to get through today," I would promise myself, "and tomorrow I will change."

My actions were shared by all the people I knew during that period. We were all alcoholics, and we all promised ourselves, "Tomorrow … tomorrow …," believing that when the next day arrived we would do whatever was necessary to change our lives, to stop drinking and get a job, to reconnect with family, to earn back our dignity and identity. We honestly believed we would do these things until we woke up the next day, and said, once again, "Tomorrow, I'll change …"

It reminds me of a sign I saw in an Irish bar when I frequented such places. Elaborately crafted and displayed, the sign read: FREE BEER TOMORROW! It didn't take a comedian to recognize that the sign would always remain in place, and that the bartender would say to a thirsty patron from the day before, "It doesn't say 'Free beer today.' It says 'Free beer *tomorrow*'!"

The inability of many people to change their reaction to a personal crisis, compounded by their difficulty in accepting the change that eventually occurs, brings to mind both the humor behind the sign and an alcoholic's response to the need for change, promising to do it tomorrow. The former is amusing. The latter is tragic. Change, especially in the middle of a crisis, takes more than telling yourself that you are assuming a new attitude or becoming a new person. It requires you to follow a proven means of dealing with your crisis, not as someone whose mental faculties are numbed by the trauma he or she is enduring, but by over-riding the inability to take action with a clear and focused mind.

One more time: *Crisis means change.* You cannot deal with your personal crisis without accepting that it involves changing some aspect of your behavior and perhaps your life.

We are resistant to change for various reasons, most of them linked to human evolution and social pressures. So change is not an easy thing to achieve, especially if the need for change confronts us unexpectedly.

*Do the Next Right Thing* has managed, I hope, to assist you in dealing with the emotional stress you may undergo during a personal crisis, and with adapting to new aspects of your life as you emerge from it. I hope you will share what you have learned among those you care for when they encounter their own crises.

I know of no more important role in life than to assist others in abandoning their suffering and finding joy in the happiness that we all deserve each day of our lives. I hope I have helped you in seeking the happiness you deserve ... and that you now feel equipped and empowered to assist others in any way you can.